easy to make!
Christmas

D1379126

Good Housekeeping

easy to make!
Christmas

COLLINS & BROWN

First published in Great Britain in 2008
by Collins & Brown
10 Southcombe Street
London W14 0RA

An imprint of Anova Books Company Ltd

The Good Housekeeping website is
www.goodhousekeeping.co.uk

1 2 3 4 5 6 7 8 9

ISBN 978-1-84340-463-7

A catalogue record for this book is available from the British
Library.

Reproduction by Dot Gradations Ltd
Printed and bound by SNP Leefung, China

This book can be ordered direct from the publisher. Contact the
marketing department, but try your bookshop first.

www.anovabooks.com

NOTES

- Both metric and imperial measures are given for the recipes. Follow either set of measures, not a mixture of both, as they are not interchangeable.
- All spoon measures are level.
  1 tsp = 5ml spoon; 1 tbsp = 15ml spoon.
- Ovens and grills must be preheated to the specified temperature.
- Use sea salt and freshly ground black pepper unless otherwise suggested.
- Fresh herbs should be used unless dried herbs are specified in a recipe.
- Medium eggs should be used except where otherwise specified. Free-range eggs are recommended.
- Note that certain recipes, including mayonnaise, lemon curd and some cold desserts, contain raw or lightly cooked eggs. The young, elderly, pregnant women and anyone with an immune-deficiency disease should avoid these, because of the slight risk of salmonella.
- Calorie, fat and carbohydrate counts per serving are provided for the recipes.

Picture Credits
Photographers: Nicki Dowey; Craig Robertson (pages 12, 14, 18, 20, 21, 24, 25); Lucinda Symons (page 28)
Stylist: Helen Trent
Home Economists: Emma Jane Frost, Lucy McKelvie

Contents

Foreword

Expectations run high once a year when it's (usually) left to just one person to provide a fantastic feast for all the family. Christmas Day – with the turkey and trimmings, cake and pudding – is the main event, and then there are all the other meals to consider. Christmas Eve needs to be special enough to signify that the celebrations have begun, but not so rich as to overshadow the next day's festivities. And there are plenty of other occasions for entertaining, from drinks parties to suppers with friends.

This book has everything you need to keep you sane and sorted. Armed with the time planner, Christmas dinner will be a breeze. I always stick a time plan to the fridge and tick things off when they're done – that way it's easy to see what stage I'm up to. We also include lots of tips for getting ahead and time-saving tricks for when the pressure's on, plus everything you need to know about turkey.

All in all we've gathered lots of ways to make your Christmas easy – and delicious. All the recipes are triple-tested in the Good Housekeeping kitchens to guarantee they work every time. We promise you that many will become firm favourites and become part of your family traditions for years to come.

Emma

Emma Marsden
Cookery Editor
Good Housekeeping

The Basics

Christmas made easy

Every year you say it will be different, promising to be more organised – and now it will be. With our roundup of the best get-ahead tips, time-saving tricks, seasonal menus and a Christmas Day countdown you'll have no excuse not to have a merry Christmas.

Make a plan

Start off by making a list of who you have invited for which meals over the festive season. Think about seating space, chairs, pans, china and cutlery – if you don't have enough, you can always borrow them from neighbours and friends, or hire them.

Next, begin to plan what you are going to cook. Refer to the Menu Planner (page 27) for suggestions. Once you've decided on the food, think about what you can prepare ahead and make your shopping lists.

You'll also need to think about drinks (see page 26). Many supermarkets and wine merchants offer online shopping and home delivery, so take advantage of this service.

Get ahead

Once you've written out your main menu plans you can start to get ahead. One of the great things about Christmas entertaining is that there is so much you can prepare and freeze in advance. The cake and pudding are best made in November, while many of the vegetables and trimmings can be frozen for up to one month. Set aside a day at the beginning of December to clear out your freezer and start restocking for Christmas. Throughout December, stock up on soft drinks, nuts, pickles and chutneys, as well as kitchen essentials such as foil, clingfilm and cocktail sticks. Don't you feel more relaxed already?

Edible gifts

If you have a spare afternoon in the week before Christmas, why not make some batches of fudge (see page 115), truffles (see page 113) or Spiced Star Biscuits (see page 109) to give as presents? Wrap in greaseproof paper or cellophane, then in ribbon-tied boxes and label with an eat-by date.

Cook's Tips

If you're going to be buying a new roasting tin this year, look for one that's heavy-based and suitable for the hob, so that you can cook the gravy in it, too. And don't forget to check the dimensions of the tin, to make sure it fits into your oven.

There's really no need to buy an electric carving knife – they tend to tear the meat rather than slice it. Instead, invest in a good-quality carving knife that will be useful all year round.

Smoked salmon can be frozen for up to three months, so keep an eye out for special offers and tuck them in the freezer until you need them. Thaw overnight in the refrigerator.

Get-ahead plan

Make Christmas Cake (see page 104)	up to 3 months ahead
Make Christmas Pudding (see page 97)	up to 8 weeks ahead
Order turkey or goose	6–8 weeks ahead
Order drinks (see page 26)	4–6 weeks ahead
Prepare and freeze potatoes (see page 66)	up to a month ahead
Prepare and freeze root vegetables (see page 71)	up to a month ahead
Prepare and freeze cranberry sauce (see page 14)	up to a month ahead
Prepare and freeze stuffing (see pages 12–13)	up to a month ahead
Prepare and freeze bread sauce (see page 15)	up to a month ahead
Prepare and freeze brandy butter (see page 15)	up to a month ahead
Prepare and freeze rolls (see page 46) or bread (see page 47)	up to a month ahead
Cover the cake with marzipan (see page 21)	up to 8 days ahead
Ice and decorate the cake (see pages 22–23)	up to 7 days ahead

Stuffings

Some people like moist stuffing, cooked inside the bird, others prefer the crisper result when the stuffing is cooked in a separate dish – why not do half and half and please everyone? All these stuffings – with the exception of the wild rice stuffing – can be made a day ahead or frozen for up to one month. Thaw overnight in the refrigerator. Cook in a preheated oven, or alongside the roast.

Best-ever Sage and Onion Stuffing

To serve eight, you will need:
1 tbsp olive oil, 1 large onion, very finely chopped, 2 tbsp finely chopped fresh sage, 7 heaped tbsp fresh white breadcrumbs, 900g (2lb) pork sausagemeat, 1 medium egg yolk, salt and ground black pepper.

1 Heat the oil in a pan and gently fry the onion until soft and golden. Stir in the sage and leave to cool.

2 Set aside 1 tbsp breadcrumbs, then mix the remainder into the sausagemeat with the onions and egg yolk. Season with salt and pepper, then set aside to cool. Cover and chill overnight, or freeze.

3 To cook, put the stuffing in an ovenproof dish, sprinkle with the reserved breadcrumbs and cook at 180°C (160°C fan oven) mark 4 for 35-40 minutes until cooked through and golden.

Cook's Tip

If you want to use the mixture to stuff the neck end of a turkey, mix in all the breadcrumbs at step 2.

Sausage, Cranberry and Apple Stuffing

To serve eight, you will need:
50g (2oz) butter, 1 onion, finely chopped, 1 garlic clove, crushed, 4 pork sausages – about 275g (10oz) – skinned and broken up, 75g (3oz) dried cranberries, 2 tbsp freshly chopped parsley, 1 red eating apple, salt and black pepper.

1 Heat the butter in a pan, add the onion and cook over a medium heat for 5 minutes or until soft. Add the garlic and cook for 1 minute. Tip into a bowl and set aside to cool. Add the sausages, cranberries and parsley, then cover and chill overnight, or freeze.

2 Core and chop the apple and add it to the stuffing. Season with salt and pepper and stir well.

3 Cook in an ovenproof dish and cook at 200°C (180°C fan oven) mark 6 for 30 minutes until cooked through.

Wild Rice and Cranberry Stuffing

This stuffing is great with goose. If you have the goose giblets, use the liver for this recipe.

To serve six to eight, you will need:
125g (4oz) wild rice, 225g (8oz) streaky bacon, cut into short strips, 2 medium red onions, about 225g (8oz) total weight, finely chopped, 75g (3oz) dried cranberries, 1 medium egg, beaten, salt and ground black pepper.

1 Put the rice in a pan and cover with 900ml (1½ pints) cold water. Add ¼ tsp salt and bring to the boil. Simmer, partly covered, for 45 minutes or until the rice is cooked. Drain and leave to cool.

2 Heat a large frying pan, add the bacon and dry-fry, turning from time to time, until lightly browned. Remove the bacon with a slotted spoon and transfer to a bowl. (If you have the goose liver, cook it in the same pan for 2–3 minutes, leave to cool, then chop it finely and add it to the bacon.) Add the onions to the frying pan and cook over a low heat until soft and translucent. Add the cranberries and cook for 1–2 minutes, then add the mixture to the bacon and leave to cool completely.

3 Add the cooked rice and the egg to the bacon mixture. Season with salt and pepper, then stir thoroughly to combine. Cover and chill overnight.

4 To cook, wrap in a buttered piece of foil and cook at 200°C (180°C fan oven) mark 6 for 30–40 minutes.

Chestnut and Butternut Squash Stuffing

To serve eight, you will need:
1 tbsp olive oil, 15g (½oz) butter, 1 onion, finely chopped, 1 small butternut squash, peeled and finely chopped, 2 rosemary sprigs, finely chopped, 2 celery sticks, finely chopped, 1 firm pear, finely chopped, 200g (7oz) peeled and cooked (or vacuum-packed) chestnuts, roughly chopped, 2 slices – about 100g (3½oz) – walnut bread, cut into small cubes, salt and ground black pepper.

1 Heat the oil and butter in a pan and gently fry the onion for 10 minutes. Add the squash and rosemary and continue to cook for another 5 minutes or until everything is soft and golden. Add the celery and pear and cook for 1-2 minutes.

2 Add the chestnuts, season with salt and pepper and mix well. Add the bread, mix everything together, then set aside to cool. Cover and chill overnight, or freeze.

3 To cook, put the stuffing in a buttered ovenproof dish and cook at 200°C (180°C fan oven) mark 6 for 25–30 minutes until golden.

Fennel and Pinenut Stuffing

To serve eight, you will need:
75g (3oz) butter, 1 bunch of spring onions, sliced, 450g (1lb) fennel, roughly chopped, 4 tbsp freshly chopped tarragon, 50g (2oz) pinenuts, toasted, 150g (5oz) goat's cheese, 150g (5oz) fresh breadcrumbs, 2 medium eggs, beaten, grated zest and juice of 1 lemon.

1 Heat the butter in a pan, add the spring onions and cook for 3 minutes. Add the fennel, cook for 5 minutes, then leave to cool.

2 Add the tarragon, pinenuts, cheese, breadcrumbs, eggs, lemon zest and juice. Season with salt and pepper; mix well. Cover and chill overnight, or freeze.

3 To cook, put the stuffing in a buttered ovenproof dish and cook at 200°C (180°C fan oven) mark 6 for 30–40 minutes until golden.

The trimmings

The turkey or goose may demand most of your attention, but don't forget the classic trimmings and sauces. Cranberry Sauce, Bread Sauce and Brandy Butter can be frozen for up to one month.

Cranberry Sauce

To serve eight, you will need:
225g (8oz) fresh cranberries, grated zest and juice of 1 orange, 4 tbsp fine shred marmalade, 125g (4oz) light muscovado sugar, 50ml (2fl oz) port.

1   Put the cranberries in a pan. Add the orange zest and juice, marmalade, sugar and port. Mix together, then bring to the boil and simmer for 5-10 minutes, stirring occasionally, until thickened. Tip into a freezerproof container, cool, label and freeze for up to one month.

Red Wine Gravy

To serve eight, you will need:
juices from the roasted bird, 1 tbsp plain flour, 150ml (1/4 pint) red wine, about 1.4 litres (2 1/2 pints) Giblet Stock (see page 17), 1 tbsp fine shred marmalade.

1   Pour off all but 2 tbsp fat from the roasting tin. Put the roasting tin on the hob over a low heat.

2   Stir in the flour using a wooden spoon, scraping up the juices from the base of the tin, and cook for 2 minutes, stirring constantly.

3   Add the wine, stirring constantly, then gradually add the stock. Bring to the boil, then add the marmalade and simmer for 5-10 minutes until thick and syrupy.

Bread Sauce

To serve eight, you will need:
1 onion, quartered, 4 cloves, 2 bay leaves, 600ml (1 pint) milk, 125g (4oz) fresh white breadcrumbs, 4 tbsp double cream, 25g (1oz) butter, a little freshly grated nutmeg, salt and ground black pepper.

1 Stud each onion quarter with a clove, then put in a pan with the bay leaves and milk. Bring to the boil, take off the heat and leave to infuse for 10 minutes.

2 Use a slotted spoon to lift out the onion and bay leaves; discard. Add the breadcrumbs to the pan and bring to the boil, stirring. Simmer for 5–6 minutes.

3 Stir in the cream and butter, then add the nutmeg, salt and pepper. Spoon into a warmed serving dish and keep warm (see Cook's Tips) until ready to serve. Alternatively, tip into a freezerproof container, cool, label and freeze for up to one month.

Cook's Tips

To keep bread sauce warm without congealing, put it in a small bowl, cover with clingfilm and put this in a large bowl filled with hot water for up to 30 minutes.
Get ahead Put the sauce in an airtight container, press a damp piece of greaseproof paper on the surface to prevent a skin forming, then cool, cover and chill for up to two days.
To use Put the sauce in a small pan with 2 tbsp cream, reheat gently, then simmer for 2 minutes until piping hot.

Glazed Chipolatas

To serve eight, you will need:
450g (1lb) chipolata sausages, 3 tbsp cranberry sauce, 1 tbsp clear honey, pinch of ground ginger, 1 tbsp olive oil.

1 Preheat the oven to 200°C (180°C fan oven) mark 6. Put the sausages in a plastic container, add the cranberry sauce, honey, ginger and oil and toss together until evenly coated.

2 Spread the chipolatas on a baking sheet and cook for 30–40 minutes. Serve immediately.

Bacon-wrapped Prunes

To serve eight, you will need:
12 rashers rindless streaky bacon, 24 ready-to-eat pitted prunes, 2 tbsp olive oil.

1 Preheat the oven to 190°C (170°C fan oven) mark 5. Cut each bacon rasher in half. Roll half a rasher around each prune.

2 Put on a baking sheet and drizzle with the olive oil. Roast for 20 minutes or until the bacon is cooked and crisp.

Get Ahead

Complete step 1, put the prunes in a sealed container and chill overnight.

Brandy Butter

To serve eight to 10, you will need:
125g (4oz) unsalted butter, 125g (4oz) light muscovado sugar, sieved, 6 tbsp brandy.

1 Put the butter in a bowl and beat until very soft. Gradually beat in the sugar until very light and fluffy.

2 Beat in the brandy, a spoonful at a time. Cover and chill for at least 3 hours.

Vegetable know-how

To save space on the cooker, invest in an electric steamer or a hob-top steamer. Cook the vegetables that take the most time in the base – carrots, for example – then steam greens in the layer above.
The secret to crispy roast potatoes and parsnips is to parboil and freeze them ahead of time.
To make the most of the space in your oven, cook roast potatoes and parsnips in the same tin. Start roasting the potatoes first, then add the parsnips after 20-30 minutes.
If you find you don't have the time to prepare your vegetables, don't feel guilty, go ahead and buy them ready-prepared.

Cooking the turkey

For perfectly cooked turkey every time, follow our easy tips on preparation and roasting.

Turkey know-how

Thawing Leave a frozen turkey in its bag and thaw at a cool room temperature, not in the refrigerator. Remove any giblets as soon as they become loose. Once there are no ice crystals inside the body cavity and the legs are flexible, cover and store in the refrigerator. Cook within 24 hours.

Take the bird out of the refrigerator 45 minutes–1 hour before roasting to allow it to reach room temperature.

Cleaning Before stuffing a bird for roasting, clean it thoroughly. Put the bird in the sink and pull out and discard any loose fat with your fingers. Then run cold water through the cavity and dry the bird well using kitchen paper.

Removing the wishbone Whether or not you are going to truss the bird, it is a good idea to remove the wishbone to make stuffing and carving easier. Pull back the flap of skin at the neck end and locate the tip of the bone with a small sharp knife. Run the knife along the inside of the bone on both sides, then on the outside. Take care not to cut deep into the breast meat. Use poultry shears or sharp-pointed scissors to snip the tip of the bone from the breastbone, and pull the bone away from the breast. Snip the two ends or pull them out by hand.

Trussing It is not necessary to truss poultry before roasting it, but it gives the bird a neater shape for serving at the table. Remove the wishbone (see above). Put the wing tips under the breast and fold the neck flap on to the back of the bird. Thread a trussing needle and use it to secure the neck flap. Push a metal skewer through the

Turkey preparation times

The cooking time has been calculated for an oven temperature of 190°C (170°C fan oven) mark 5.

Oven-ready weight (at room temperature)	Approximate no. of servings
2.3–3.6kg (5–8lb)	6–10
3.6–5kg (8–11lb)	10–15
5–6.8kg (11–15lb)	15–20
6.8–9kg (15–20lb)	20–30

legs, at the joint between the thigh and drumstick. Twist some string around both ends of the skewer and pull firmly to tighten. Turn the bird over. Bring the string over the ends of the drumsticks, pull tight and tie to secure the legs.

Stuffing Loosely stuff the neck end only. Allow 225g (8oz) stuffing for each 2.3kg (5lb) weight of bird and stuff just before cooking. Secure the neck skin with skewers or cocktail sticks, or sew using a trussing needle threaded with fine string. Weigh the bird after stuffing to calculate the cooking time. Roast at 190°C (170°C fan oven) mark 5 for 20 minutes per 450g (1lb), plus 20 minutes extra.

If you find that the bird is too big for your roasting tin, slice off the legs using a carving knife. Weigh the bird again and recalculate the cooking time. Weigh the legs, calculate the cooking time, then put them in a separate roasting tin and cook under the bird.

Cooking Coat with butter and season. Wrap loosely in a 'tent' of foil, then cook in a preheated oven at 190°C (170°C fan oven) mark 5 (see chart below for timings). Remove the foil about 1 hour before the end of cooking time to brown the bird. Baste regularly.

How to tell when the turkey is cooked Pierce the thickest part of the leg with a skewer. The juices that run out should be golden and clear with no traces of pink; if they're not, return the bird to the oven and check at regular intervals.

Resting Once the bird is cooked, allow it to rest for 20-30 minutes before carving. Lift it out of the roasting tin, put it on a plate and cover with foil and a clean teatowel. This allows the juices to settle back into the meat, leaving it moist and easier to carve.

Use this chart as a guideline, but if a recipe gives a different oven temperature, follow the recipe timing.

Approximate thawing time	Cooking time (foil-wrapped)
15–18 hours	2–3 hours
18–20 hours	3–3¼ hours
20–24 hours	3¼–4 hours
24–30 hours	4–5½ hours

The finishing touches A little garnish will help to make the cooked turkey look attractive on the table. Transfer the bird to a platter, then use sprigs of fresh parsley and rosemary, tucking the stalks into the cavity of the bird.

Serving the stuffing Use a long-handled spoon to scoop out the stuffing and transfer it to a suitable serving dish.

Storing leftovers Don't forget the leftover turkey when lunch is finished – never leave it standing in a warm room. Cool it quickly in a cold place, then cover and chill.

Giblet Stock

To make 1.3 litres (2¼ pints), you will need:
turkey giblets, 1 onion, quartered, 1 carrot, halved, 1 celery stick, halved, 6 black peppercorns, 1 bay leaf.

1 Put the giblets in a large pan. Add the onion, carrot, celery, peppercorns and bay leaf. Pour in 1.4 litres (2½ pints) cold water, cover and bring to the boil.

2 Simmer for 30 minutes–1 hour, skimming occasionally. Strain through a sieve. Cool quickly, put into a sealable container and chill for up to three days.

Alternatives to turkey

Goose and duck

What to buy (oven-ready weight)	Approximate no. of servings	Cooking time (approx.)
Duck, 1.8–2.5kg (4–5½lb)	2–4	1½–2 hours
Goose, small, 4.3–5.4kg (9½–12lb)	4–7	20 minutes per 450g (1lb) at 200°C (180°C) mark 6
Goose, medium, 5.4–6.3kg (12–14lb)	8–11	25 minutes per 450g (1lb) at 200°C (180°C) mark 6

Cook's Tip

When roasting duck or goose, spoon off the excess fat every 20–30 minutes. Keep the fat in a bowl in the refrigerator: it lasts for months and is excellent for cooking roast potatoes.

Carving

1 To carve the breast, use the fork to steady the turkey. Starting at the neck end, cut long slices about 5mm (¼in) thick. Use the knife and fork to lift them on to a warmed serving plate. To remove the wing, cut through the corner of the breast until you feel the wing joint. Cut through it and serve a wing with a slice of breast. Repeat on the other side.

2 To remove the legs, use the fork to steady the turkey. Cut down through the skin between the thigh and the breast.

3 Use the flat of the knife to push the thigh out and cut through the hip joint, separating the leg. Repeat on the other side.

4 To carve meat from the leg, first separate the two parts of the leg.

5 Holding the drumstick by the thin end, stand it up on the carving board and carve slices roughly parallel with the bone. The thigh can be carved either flat on the board or upright.

The final countdown

Christmas need not be a mad panic if you've done all you can in advance, including making a cook's time plan for Christmas Day.

23 December

Make a shopping list of all the fresh food you need to buy. Make the Giblet Stock (see page 17) and chill.

24 December

Hit the shops really early, armed with your list. Aim to spend two hours shopping, ticking off every item on the list. Go home, check your meal plan to make sure you've got everything ready for tomorrow, then relax – it's Christmas!

Christmas Day time plan

Based on the Lemon and Herb Roast Turkey (see page 55), using a double oven. Lunch: 2pm. If you don't have a double oven your turkey can stand, covered in foil, for up to 1 hour while you complete the accompaniments.

Adapt this time plan to any recipe(s) you choose, slotting in puddings and accompaniments where appropriate. Work back from the time you need to serve the meal, allowing yourself enough time at every stage.

8am Take turkey out of refrigerator. Arrange racks in main oven for the turkey and extra stuffing. Preheat oven to 220°C (200°C fan oven) mark 7. Stuff and weigh turkey.

9am Cook turkey in main oven. Chill champagne and white wine.

9.30am Reduce oven temperature to 170°C (150°C fan oven) mark 3 and cook turkey for a further 3½ hours.

12pm Preheat second oven to 220°C (200°C fan oven) mark 7.

12.20pm Begin cooking potatoes in second oven.

12.35pm Put the pudding on to steam. Roast parsnips in the second oven.

1pm Increase the main oven temperature to 200°C (180°C fan oven) mark 6, remove foil from turkey and add bacon rolls and chipolatas.

1.15pm Reduce the temperature of the second oven to 200°C (180°C fan oven) mark 6 .

1.25pm Cook the extra stuffing in the main oven.

1.30pm Warm plates and serving dishes. Reheat red cabbage.

1.40pm Take turkey out of oven. Put on to warm platter. Make gravy.

1.45pm Cook sprouts, put into serving dishes and keep warm. Reheat bread and cranberry sauces. Put into serving dishes and keep warm.

1.50pm Put everything else into warm serving dishes.

2pm Lunch is served! Check the water level on the Christmas pudding before you sit down to eat.

Lining tins

Round tin

1 Put the tin on a sheet of greaseproof paper and draw a circle around its circumference. Cut out the circle just inside the drawn line.

2 Cut a strip or strips about 2cm (³⁄₄in) wider than the depth of the tin and fold up one long edge of each strip by 1cm (¹⁄₂in). Make cuts, about 2.5cm (1in) apart, through the folded edge of the strip(s) up to the fold line.

3 Lightly grease the tin with butter, making sure it is completely coated. Press the strip(s) on to the sides of the tin so that the snipped edge sits on the base.

4 Lay the circle in the bottom of the tin and grease the paper.

Baking and decorating the cake

For the easiest-ever Christmas Cake recipe, turn to page 104; use these tips and techniques to guide you through the preparation process. If you haven't time to make a cake, buy an un-iced cake and choose one of our decorating ideas on pages 22–23.

Square tin

1 Cut out a square of greaseproof paper slightly smaller than the base of the tin. Cut four strips about 2cm (³/₄in) wider than the depth of the tin and fold up one of the longest edges of each strip by 1cm (¹/₂in).

2 Lightly grease the tin with butter, making sure it is coated on all sides and in the corners.

3 Cut one strip to the length of the side of the tin and press into place, with the narrow folded section sitting on the base. Continue, cutting to fit into the corners, to cover all four sides.

4 Lay the square on the base of the tin, then grease the paper, taking care not to move the side strips.

Using marzipan

Christmas cakes need to be covered with marzipan before they are iced, to prevent the icing from discolouring.

For a 20.5cm (8in) round or 18cm (7in) square cake, you will need:
4 tbsp apricot jam, icing sugar to dust, 500g (1lb 2oz) marzipan.

1 Put the cake on a board or serving plate. Heat the jam in a small pan with 1 tbsp water over a low heat, stirring until smooth. Sieve into a small bowl, then brush all over the cake.

2 Dust the worksurface with sifted icing sugar, roll out the marzipan to a 38cm (15in) round. Lift the marzipan over the cake, smooth out from the centre and down the sides, then trim away any excess. Leave in a cool dry place for 24 hours before icing.

Baking Tips

Buy cake boards and Christmas cake decorations in November.

To make sure the greaseproof paper peels off the cake once it's cooked, brush it with sunflower oil or melted butter. Do not use baking parchment, as it's non-stick and will cause your cake to shrink away from the side of the tin, which could make it an irregular shape. Don't grease the paper too thickly – this 'fries' the edges of the cake.

Christmas cake should keep for three months. Make sure you wrap it in clingfilm, then in foil and store in an airtight container, to prevent it from drying out.

If you don't have a turntable for decorating your Christmas cake, put it on a board on top of a sturdy can to allow you to turn the cake with one hand as you decorate it.

Marzipan (almond paste) is not suitable for freezing, as it dulls the flavour and makes the marzipan sticky and difficult to roll out.

Marzipan the cake about a week before Christmas, so it has time to dry out before you ice it.

Ice the cake up to a week before Christmas.

Snowflake Cake

For an 18cm (7in) square or 20.5cm (8in) round cake, you will need:
2 x 300g tubs ready-made royal icing, piping bag with small plain nozzle, icing sugar to dust, 1m (40in) silver string.

1 Spoon 3 tbsp of the icing into the piping bag. Spoon the remaining icing on top of the cake and use a palette knife to spread over the top and sides in an even layer, swirling the icing with the knife

2 Using the icing in the piping bag, mark six points, spaced at equal distances apart, towards the outer edge of the top of the cake; use these points as a guideline to pipe a snowflake pattern. Leave the icing to dry overnight.

3 Dust the cake with icing sugar and tie the string around the cake, finishing with a bow.

Frosted Fruit

Frosted berries make a beautiful contrasting decoration for dark or white iced cakes.

You will need:
fresh cranberries or redcurrants, fresh bay or holly leaves, 1 medium egg white, lightly beaten, 25g (1oz) caster sugar.

1 Brush the berries and leaves lightly with beaten egg white. Spread the sugar on a tray, making sure there are no lumps. Dip the berries and leaves into the sugar, shake off any excess, then leave to dry on a tray lined with greaseproof paper or baking parchment for about 1 hour.

Penguin Cake

For a 20.5cm (8in) round cake, you will need:
icing sugar to dust, 750g (1lb 11oz) ready-to-roll white icing, 1 pack multicoloured icing, edible silver balls, 70cm (28in) ribbon.

1 Dust the worksurface with icing sugar and roll out the icing to a 38cm (15in) round. Use the rolling pin to lift the icing and drape it over the cake; smooth into place. Reserve the trimmings.

2 To make the penguins, take a small piece of black icing and roll into an egg shape. Roll a small piece of the reserved white icing into a ball and flatten into an oval. Mould the oval around the front of the penguin's body. Roll a small piece of black icing into a ball and place on top of the body, moulding it to form the head. Make two small holes for the eyes using a cocktail stick. Shape a small piece of red icing into a cone shape and press gently on to the head to form a beak. Using a sharp knife or scalpel, cut each side, about a quarter of the way from the top, and pull each side out to form the penguin's wings. Roll out a small piece of red icing and cut out two ovals for the feet; press gently on to the body. Repeat this process to make six more different-sized penguins.

3 To make a scarf, roll out a piece of coloured icing, cut a long thin strip and place around the penguin's neck. To make a hat, roll out a small thin circle of coloured icing, carefully push a small hollow in the centre and place on the penguin's head. Add a contrasting bobble and press gently in place.

4 Arrange the penguins on top of the cake. Scatter silver balls around the penguins and dust with icing sugar to give a snowy effect. Fix the ribbon around the cake and secure with sticky tape.

Cook's Tip

For a dramatic effect, just before serving, push 4–6 mini sparklers into the cake. These burn down very quickly, so ask someone to help you light them all at the same time.

Star Cake

See picture on page 20.

For a 20.5cm (8in) round cake, you will need:
icing sugar to dust, 1kg (2¼lb) ready-to-roll white icing, star cutters, edible silver balls, 70cm (28in) ribbon.

1 Dust the worksurface with icing sugar. Use 1 pack of icing to make the stars. Roll out to 5mm (¼in) thick. Use star cutters to cut out 20–30 stars. Leave to dry on a wire rack for 24 hours.
Note: this can be done at the same time as the marzipan is drying.

2 Dust the worksurface with icing sugar. Put the remaining packs of icing together and roll out to a 38cm (15in) round. Use the rolling pin to lift the icing and drape it over the cake; smooth into place.

3 Arrange the stars on the cake, along with the silver balls. Fix the ribbon around the cake and secure with sticky tape.

2 **3**

Preparing pineapple

1 Cut off the base and crown of the pineapple, and stand the fruit on a chopping board. Using a medium-sized knife, cut away a section of skin, going just deep enough to remove all or most of the hard, inedible 'eyes'. Repeat all the way around.

2 Use a small knife to cut out any remaining traces of eyes.

3 Cut the peeled pineapple into slices. You can buy special tools for coring pineapples but a 7.5cm (3in) biscuit cutter or an apple corer works just as well. Place the biscuit cutter directly over the core and press down firmly. If using an apple corer, cut out the core in pieces, as it will be too wide to remove in one piece.

1

Fruit

Amid all the rich food of the festive season, fresh fruit makes a refreshing dessert, served individually or combined in a fruit salad.

2 **3**

Preparing mangoes

1 Cut a slice to one side of the stone in the centre. Repeat on the other side.

2 Cut parallel lines into the flesh of one slice, almost to the skin. Cut another set of lines to cut the flesh into squares.

3 Press on the skin side to turn the fruit inside out, so that the flesh is thrust outwards. Cut off the chunks as close as possible to the skin. Repeat with the other half.

Segmenting citrus fruit

1 Cut off a slice at both ends of the fruit, then cut off the peel, just inside the white pith.

2 Hold the fruit over a bowl to catch the juice and cut between the segments, just inside the membrane, to release the flesh. Continue until all the segments are removed. Squeeze the juice from the membrane into the bowl and use as required.

Papaya with Lime Syrup

To serve four, you will need:
75g (3oz) golden caster sugar, zest and juice of 2 limes, 2 papayas, peeled, halved and seeds removed.

1 Put the sugar in a small pan with 100ml (3½fl oz) water and the lime zest and juice. Heat gently to dissolve the sugar, then bring to the boil and bubble rapidly for 5 minutes or until the mixture is reduced and syrupy.

2 Cut the papayas into slices and arrange on a large serving plate. Drizzle over the lime syrup and serve.

Exotic Fruit Salad

To serve four, you will need:
2 oranges, 1 mango, peeled, stoned and chopped, 450g (1lb) peeled and diced fresh pineapple, ½ Charentais melon, cubed, 200g (7oz) blueberries, grated zest and juice of 1 lime.

1 Using a sharp knife, peel the oranges, remove the pith and cut into segments. Put into a bowl.

2 Add the mango to the bowl with the pineapple, melon and blueberries.

3 Add the lime zest and juice, and gently mix together. Serve immediately.

Try Something Different

Use 2 papayas, peeled, seeded and chopped, instead of the pineapple. Mix the seeds of 2 passion fruit with the lime juice before adding to the salad.

- Choose a wine that's not too high in alcohol – don't go higher than 13% alcohol by volume.

- If you don't have enough glasses, consider hiring them, rather than buying plastic glasses. Most supermarkets and off-licences offer a free service – just make sure you order in good time and return them clean and undamaged. Ask at the store's customer service desk.

- Cool wine quickly in an ice bath – use half ice and half water and put the bottles in to chill for 20 minutes. If you've bought drinks on a sale-or-return basis, remember to put the bottles in a black bin liner before you chill them, securing it tightly so that the bottles stay dry and the labels don't slip off.

- When pouring red or white wine into a glass, only fill the glass one-third to half full at the most. For a red wine, this allows the drinker to swirl it around the glass and aerate it, while, for a white, pouring just a small amount at a time prevents the wine from warming up too quickly in the glass.

Wine and drinks guide

Christmas isn't Christmas without drinks on hand to provide some festive cheer.

Wine

You'll need a supply of good everyday whites and reds that can complement a range of dishes to see you through the holiday. If you're entertaining in numbers, you'll need to order by the case.

- Allow one bottle of wine per head, which roughly works out to six glasses each. It's better to have too much than too little. You can buy wine on a sale-or-return basis – check with your local supermarket or off-licence – but to go back, the bottles must be unopened and in a saleable condition.

Champagne

There's nothing like a glass of chilled champagne to get the Christmas morning festivities going with a swing. It's also a great way to kick off a party. You can usually save money by buying in bulk.

- Chill champagne for as long as possible. The lower the temperature, the lower the pressure in the bottle, so the cork is less likely to fly off.

- To avoid champagne spilling over as you pour it into flutes, pour a little into a glass first, swirl it, then tip it into the next one. If the glass is wet, less fizz bubbles up.

Non-alcoholic drinks

Make sure you have plenty of soft drinks on hand for those who are driving, pregnant or simply don't drink alcohol (and don't forget the children). Stock up on a range of fruit juices, lemonade, tonic and sparkling water. Try serving a fruit punch made from orange juice, cranberry juice and tonic on ice.

Menu planner

Christmas is the time to catch up with family and friends. We've put together a few menu suggestions for different occasions.

Festive drinks party

Champagne Cocktail
Cranberry Crush
Cranberry Cooler (non-alcoholic)
☆ ☆ ☆
Lemon and Rosemary Olives
Chilli-roasted Nuts and Raisins
Cocktail Rolls
Mozzarella Nibbles
Deli Bites
Hot-smoked Salmon Blinis
Chorizo Chicken

How many nibbles do I need?

As a guideline, allow 5 canapés per person per hour. If you're serving nibbles with pre-dinner drinks for 8 people, make 40 nibbles. For a drinks party for 20 people lasting 3 hours, make 300. Don't forget to make plenty of mince pies to offer your guests.

Christmas Eve supper for 6

Red Onion and Gorgonzola Salad
☆ ☆ ☆
Spinach and Smoked Salmon Tart
Roasted Stuffed Peppers
   (vegetarian)
☆ ☆ ☆
Oranges with Caramel Sauce

Traditional Christmas lunch for 8

Quick Salmon Mousse
☆ ☆ ☆
Lemon and Herb Roast Turkey
Red Wine Gravy
Crispy Roast Potatoes
Spicy Roasted Roots
Brussels Sprouts with Pancetta
Braised Red Cabbage
Cranberry Sauce
Bread Sauce
☆ ☆ ☆
Christmas Pudding and Brandy
   Butter
Tropical Fruit and Coconut Trifle

Classic Christmas lunch for 8

Smoked Salmon and Scallop Parcels
☆ ☆ ☆
Roast Goose with Wild Rice and
   Cranberry Stuffing
Red Wine Gravy
Crispy Roast Potatoes
Lemon and Orange Carrots
Braised Red Cabbage
☆ ☆ ☆
Christmas Pudding and Brandy
   Butter
☆ ☆ ☆
Champagne Jellies

Vegetarian Christmas lunch for 8

Watercress Soup
☆ ☆ ☆
Nut and Cranberry Terrine
Crispy Roast Potatoes
Spicy Roasted Roots
Spinach with Tomatoes
☆ ☆ ☆
Christmas Pudding and Brandy
   Butter
Drunken Pears

Boxing Day buffet for 15–20

Roasted Salmon
Ginger and Honey-glazed Ham
Festive Salad
Mixed Beans with Lemon
   Vinaigrette
☆ ☆ ☆
Stollen
Mince Pies
Spiced Star Biscuits
Tropical Fruit and Coconut Trifle

Supper for 6

Sweet Chilli Prawns
☆ ☆ ☆
Spiced Leg of Lamb
Baked Potatoes with Mustard Seeds
Festive Salad
☆ ☆ ☆
Cognac and Crème Fraîche
   Ice Cream

Vegetarian supper for 6

Mozzarella Nibbles (omit the ham)
☆ ☆ ☆
Artichoke and Mushroom Lasagne
Winter Coleslaw
☆ ☆ ☆
Cognac and Crème Fraîche
   Ice Cream
Mince Pies

New Year's Eve supper for 6

Salmon and Asparagus Terrine (with
   some left over for lunch)
☆ ☆ ☆
Fillet of Beef en Croûte
Spinach with Tomatoes
Lemon and Orange Carrots
☆ ☆ ☆
Champagne Jellies

Food storage and hygiene

Storing food properly and preparing it in a hygienic way is important to ensure that it remains as nutritious and flavourful as possible, and to reduce the risk of food poisoning. Food hygiene is especially important at Christmas, particularly if you are feeding the very young, pregnant or elderly.

Hygiene

When you are preparing food, always follow these important guidelines:

Wash your hands thoroughly before handling food and again between handling different types of food, such as raw and cooked meat and poultry. If you have any cuts or grazes on your hands, be sure to keep them covered with a waterproof plaster.

Wash down worksurfaces regularly with a mild detergent solution or multi-surface cleaner.

Use a dishwasher if available. Otherwise, wear rubber gloves for washing-up, so that the water temperature can be hotter than unprotected hands can bear. Wash and change drying-up cloths and cleaning cloths regularly. Note that leaving dishes to drain is more hygienic than drying them with a teatowel.

Keep raw and cooked foods separate, especially meat, fish and poultry. Wash kitchen utensils in between preparing raw and cooked foods. Never put cooked or ready-to-eat foods directly on to a surface which has just had raw fish, meat or poultry on it.

Keep pets out of the kitchen if possible; or make sure they stay away from worksurfaces. Never allow animals on to worksurfaces.

Shopping

Always choose fresh ingredients in prime condition from stores and markets that have a regular turnover of stock to ensure you buy the freshest produce possible.

Make sure items are within their 'best before' or 'use by' date. (Foods with a longer shelf life have a 'best before' date; more perishable items have a 'use by' date.)

Pack frozen and chilled items in an insulated cool bag at the check-out and put them in the freezer or refrigerator as soon as you get home.

During warm weather in particular, buy perishable foods just before you return home. When packing items at the check-out, sort them according to where you will store them when you get home – the refrigerator, freezer, storecupboard, vegetable rack, fruit bowl, etc. This will make unpacking easier – and quicker.

The storecupboard

Although storecupboard ingredients will generally last a long time, correct storage is important.

Always check packaging for storage advice – even with familiar foods, because storage requirements may change if additives, sugar or salt have been reduced. Check storecupboard foods for their 'best before' or 'use by' date and do not use them if the date has passed.

Keep all food cupboards scrupulously clean and make sure food containers and packets are properly sealed.

Once opened, treat canned foods as though fresh. Always transfer the contents to a clean container, cover and keep in the refrigerator. Similarly, jars, sauce bottles and cartons should be kept chilled after opening. (Check the label for safe storage times after opening.)

Transfer dry goods such as flour, sugar, rice and pasta to airtight moisture-proof containers. When supplies are used up, wash the container well and dry thoroughly before refilling with new supplies.

Store oils in a dark cupboard away from any heat source as heat and light can make them turn rancid and affect their colour. For the same reason, buy olive oil in dark green bottles.

Store vinegars in a cool place; they can turn bad in a warm environment.

Store dried herbs, spices and flavourings in a cool, dark cupboard or in dark jars. Buy in small quantities as their flavour will not last indefinitely.

Refrigerator storage

Fresh food needs to be kept in the cool temperature of the refrigerator to keep it in good condition and discourage the growth of harmful bacteria. Store day-to-day perishable items, such as opened jams and jellies, mayonnaise and bottled sauces, in the refrigerator along with eggs and dairy products, fruit juices, bacon, fresh and cooked meat (on separate shelves), and salads and vegetables (except potatoes, which don't suit being stored in the cold). A refrigerator should be kept at an operating temperature of 4–5°C.

It is worth investing in a refrigerator thermometer to ensure the correct temperature is maintained. To ensure your refrigerator is functioning effectively for safe food storage, follow these guidelines:

To avoid bacterial cross-contamination, store cooked and raw foods on separate shelves, putting cooked foods on the top shelf. Ensure that all items are well wrapped.

Never put hot food into the refrigerator, as this will cause the internal temperature of the refrigerator to rise.

Avoid overfilling the refrigerator, as this restricts the circulation of air and can prevent the appliance from working properly.

It can take some time for the refrigerator to return to the correct operating temperature once the door has been opened, so don't leave it open any longer than is necessary.

Clean the refrigerator regularly, using a specially formulated germicidal refrigerator cleaner. Alternatively, use a weak solution of bicarbonate of soda: 1 tbsp to 1 litre (1^3/$_4$ pints) water.

If your refrigerator doesn't have an automatic defrost facility, defrost regularly.

Maximum refrigerator storage times

For pre-packed foods, always adhere to the 'use by' date on the packet. For other foods, the following storage times should apply, providing the food is in prime condition when it goes into the refrigerator and that your refrigerator is in good working order.

Vegetables and Fruit

Green vegetables	3–4 days
Salad leaves	2–3 days
Hard and stone fruit	3–7 days
Soft fruit	1–2 days

Dairy Food

Cheese, hard	1 week
Cheese, soft	2–3 days
Eggs	1 week
Milk	4–5 days

Fish

Fish	1 day
Shellfish	1 day

Raw Meat

Bacon	7 days
Game	2 days
Joints	3 days
Poultry	2 days
Raw sliced meat	2 days
Sausages	3 days

Cooked Meat

Joints	3 days
Casseroles/stews	2 days
Pies	2 days
Sliced meat	2 days
Ham	2 days
Ham, vacuum-packed (or according to the instructions on the packet)	1–2 weeks

1

Party Food

Cook's Tip

Don't waste the flavoured oil left over from the olives. It's perfect for using in salad dressings and marinades.

Lemon and Rosemary Olives

a few fresh rosemary sprigs, plus extra to decorate

1 garlic clove

175g (6oz) mixed black and green Greek olives

pared zest of 1 lemon

2 tbsp vodka (optional)

300ml (½ pint) extra virgin olive oil

1 Put the rosemary and garlic in a small heatproof bowl and pour over enough boiling water to cover. Leave for 1–2 minutes, then drain well.

2 Put the olives, lemon zest and vodka, if using, in a glass jar and add the rosemary and garlic. Pour over enough olive oil to cover the olives. Cover and chill for at least 24 hours before using.

3 To serve, remove the olives from the oil and decorate with sprigs of fresh rosemary. Use within one week.

Serves 6	EASY		NUTRITIONAL INFORMATION	
	Preparation Time 15 minutes, plus at least 24 hours chilling		**Per Serving** 300 calories, 36g fat (of which 5g saturates), 0g carbohydrate, 1.2g salt	Vegetarian Gluten free • Dairy free

Chilli-roasted Nuts and Raisins

220g pack mixed unsalted nuts, seeds and raisins, unroasted

1 tsp ground paprika

a large pinch of dried crushed chilli flakes

2 tsp olive oil

fine sea salt

1 Preheat the oven to 200°C (180°C fan oven) mark 6. Put the nuts, seeds and raisins in a small bowl and stir in the paprika, chilli flakes and olive oil.

2 Tip the nuts on to an edged baking sheet and season lightly with salt. Roast in the oven, stirring occasionally, for 12–15 minutes until golden and toasted. Serve warm or cool. Store in an airtight container for up to five days.

EASY		NUTRITIONAL INFORMATION		Serves
Preparation Time 3 minutes	**Cooking Time** 12–15 minutes	**Per Serving** 169 calories, 11g fat (of which 2g saturates), 14g carbohydrate, 0.2g salt	Vegetarian Gluten free • Dairy free	**6**

Cocktail Rolls

200g (7oz) smoked salmon slices
100g (3½oz) full-fat soft cheese or goat's cheese
1 tbsp dill-flavoured mustard or creamed horseradish
1 large courgette
about 2 tbsp hummus
200g (7oz) prosciutto (see Cook's Tip)
about 2 tbsp fruity chutney, such as mango
1 small bunch of chives, finely chopped
1 roasted red pepper, finely chopped
ground black pepper

1 Lay the smoked salmon on a sheet of greaseproof paper. Spread with a thin layer of cheese, then a layer of mustard or horseradish, and roll up.

2 Using a vegetable peeler, pare the courgette into long, wafer-thin strips. Lay the strips on a board, spread with cheese, then hummus, and roll up.

3 Lay the prosciutto on a board. Spread thinly with cheese, then with the chutney, and roll up.

4 Stand the rolls on a greaseproof paper-lined baking sheet (trimming bases if necessary), cover with clingfilm and chill for up to 8 hours.

5 About 2 minutes before serving, top each roll with a little cheese. Dip the salmon rolls into the chopped chives, the prosciutto rolls into the red pepper and the courgette rolls into coarsely ground black pepper.

Cook's Tip

Prosciutto is Italian dry-cured ham. It is available from Italian delis and most supermarkets. Parma ham is a type of prosciutto, but other types are less expensive.

EASY	NUTRITIONAL INFORMATION		Serves
Preparation Time 20 minutes	**Per Serving** 117 calories, 7g fat (of which 3g saturates), 4g carbohydrate, 1.7g salt	Gluten free	**10**

Cook's Tips

Bocconcini are mini mozzarella balls – the perfect bite-size nibble. They are available from Italian delis and good supermarkets. Alternatively, replace with two regular mozzarella balls, cubed.
For vegetarians, omit the ham.
Instead of artichokes use halved cherry tomatoes.

Mozzarella Nibbles

2 x 125g tubs bocconcini, drained (see Cook's Tips)
75g (3oz) thinly sliced Parma ham, cut into strips
400g (14oz) pitted black and green olives, halved
125g (4oz) roasted artichokes, cut into small pieces
125g (4oz) roasted peppers, cut into small pieces
1 bunch of basil leaves

1 Wrap each mozzarella ball in a piece of Parma ham. Push a halved olive on to a cocktail stick, then add a piece of artichoke, a piece of pepper, a basil leaf, then a wrapped mozzarella ball. Repeat to make about 30 nibbles. Serve immediately or cover and chill for up to 1 hour.

Makes 30	EASY		NUTRITIONAL INFORMATION	
	Preparation Time 15 minutes		Per Canapé 41 calories, 3g fat (of which 1g saturates), 1g carbohydrate, 0.9g salt	Gluten free

Cook's Tips

Tapenade is a black olive paste from Provence in the south of France. You can buy ready-made tapenade or make your own by whizzing 75g (3oz) pitted black olives in a food processor with 4 anchovies, 2 tbsp olive oil and 1 tbsp freshly chopped flat-leafed parsley.

Instead of spreading it on bread, serve tapenade as a dip for crisp raw carrots, red pepper strips or chicory leaves.

Bruschetta with Tapenade

1 ciabatta loaf

olive oil to brush

6 tbsp tapenade (see Cook's Tips)

selection of vegetable antipasti, such as marinated red peppers and artichokes, drained

a few basil sprigs to garnish

1 Cut the ciabatta on the diagonal to make 12 slices. Brush both sides of the slices with a little olive oil. Heat a griddle pan until hot, add the ciabatta slices and toast for a couple of minutes on each side.

2 Spread a thin layer of tapenade on each slice of bread, then top with a little of the antipasti. Garnish with basil and serve. Alternatively, arrange the antipasti in separate bowls and let your guests assemble their own bruschettas.

EASY		NUTRITIONAL INFORMATION		Makes
Preparation Time 10 minutes	**Cooking Time** 5 minutes	**Per Slice** 119 calories, 4g fat (of which trace saturates), 19g carbohydrate, 0.7g salt	Dairy free	**12**

Deli Bites

2 large slices of day-old bread
25g (1oz) garlic or herb butter, softened

For the guacamole and bacon topping
100g (3½oz) guacamole
50g (2oz) crispy cooked streaky bacon, finely chopped
a few fresh coriander leaves

For the goat's cheese and salsa topping
75g (3oz) medium-fat soft goat's cheese
75g (3oz) chunky tomato salsa
50g (2oz) pitted black olives, chopped

1 Preheat the oven to 180°C (160°C fan oven) mark 4. Thinly spread each slice of bread with the garlic butter, then remove the crusts. Now cut each slice into quarters, then cut each quarter into four triangles or squares to make 32 bite-size pieces.

2 Divide the pieces of bread, butter side up, between two baking sheets and bake for 25 minutes until crisp and pale golden. Remove from the oven and leave to cool completely.

3 Up to three hours ahead, spoon guacamole on to half the bites, then sprinkle with chopped bacon. Spread the remaining bites with goat's cheese, top with salsa, then sprinkle with chopped olives. Cover loosely with clingfilm and chill until ready to serve.

4 Just before serving, snip fresh coriander leaves over the guacamole bites.

Get Ahead

To prepare ahead Complete the recipe to the end of step 2; store in an airtight container for up to five days.

Makes	EASY		NUTRITIONAL INFORMATION
32	**Preparation Time** 20 minutes	**Cooking Time** 25 minutes	**Per Canapé** Guacamole: 30 calories, 3g fat (of which 1g saturates), 1g carbohydrate, 0.2g salt Goat's cheese: 31 calories, 2g fat (of which 1g saturates), 1g carbohydrate, 0.3g salt

Try Something Different

Use fresh coriander instead of basil.
Instead of prawns, use cooked and peeled crayfish tails.

Sweet Chilli Prawns

30 cooked peeled large prawns, about 250g (9oz)
150ml bottle sweet chilli sauce
grated zest and juice of ½ lime
3 tbsp freshly chopped basil
½ cucumber, about 15cm (6in) long
2 tbsp clear honey

1 The night before you want to serve this recipe, put the prawns, 2 tbsp of the chilli sauce, the lime zest and juice and the basil in a small bowl. Stir gently to mix, then cover the bowl with clingfilm and chill overnight.

2 Up to three hours before serving, use a vegetable peeler to pare along the length of the cucumber to make 15 thin strips. Cut each cucumber strip in half widthways.

3 Thread each piece of cucumber on to a cocktail stick in a concertina shape, then add a prawn. Cover the skewers with clingfilm and chill until ready to serve.

4 To serve, spoon the remaining chilli sauce into a small serving bowl and stir in the honey. Pile the prawn and cucumber skewers on to a large serving plate and serve with the chilli sauce for dipping.

Makes 30	EASY		NUTRITIONAL INFORMATION	
	Preparation Time 20 minutes, plus overnight marinating		**Per Canapé** 16 calories, trace fat, 1g carbohydrate, 0.1g salt	Gluten free • Dairy free

Cook's Tips

Originally from Russia, blinis are bite-size pancakes made with a yeast batter; they can be topped with a variety of ingredients to make perfect party canapés. Available from most supermarkets.

Instead of blinis, use small pieces of pumpernickel or rye bread.

Instead of hot-smoked salmon, use thinly sliced smoked salmon. Spread crème fraîche on to the blinis, then fold the salmon loosely on top. Sprinkle with chives and serve with lemon wedges to squeeze over.

Hot-smoked Salmon Blinis

125g (4oz) hot-smoked salmon flakes

3 tbsp crème fraîche

16 small blinis or 125g pack (see Cook's Tips)

1 tbsp freshly snipped chives

ground black pepper

1 Put the salmon flakes, crème fraîche and a little ground black pepper in a bowl and mix gently. Put 1 tsp of the mixture on to each blini, sprinkle with chopped chives and serve immediately.

EASY	NUTRITIONAL INFORMATION	Makes
Preparation Time 5 minutes	**Per Blini** 43 calories, 3g fat (of which 1g saturates), 2g carbohydrate, 0.3g salt	**16**

Try Something Different

Use mini poppadoms instead of croustades.
Replace the chutney with cranberry sauce.
Instead of roast chicken, use turkey.

Tangy Chicken Bites

2 x 50g packs mini croustades

about 275g (10oz) fruity chutney, such as mango

2 roast chicken breasts, skinned, torn into small pieces

250g carton crème fraîche

a few fresh thyme sprigs

1   Place the croustades on a board. Spoon about ½ tsp chutney into each one. Top with a few shreds of chicken, a small dollop of crème fraîche and a few thyme leaves. Transfer the croustades to a large serving plate and serve immediately.

Makes 48	EASY	NUTRITIONAL INFORMATION
	Preparation Time 10 minutes	**Per Canapé** 43 calories, 2g fat (of which 1g saturates), 4g carbohydrate, 0.1g salt

Try Something Different

Replace the chicken with 24 large raw peeled prawns; cook for 5 minutes until the prawns turn pink.

Chorizo Chicken

200g (7oz) skinless, boneless chicken breast, cut into 24 bite-size pieces
100g (3½oz) thinly sliced chorizo
24 fresh sage leaves
12 cherry tomatoes, halved

1 Preheat the oven to 190°C (170°C fan oven) mark 5. Spread the chicken pieces on a board and top each with a slice of chorizo, a sage leaf and half a cherry tomato. Secure with cocktail sticks.

2 Place on a baking sheet and cook for 10 minutes or until the chicken is cooked through. Transfer the chicken and chorizo skewers to a serving plate and serve warm.

EASY		NUTRITIONAL INFORMATION		Makes
Preparation Time 10 minutes	**Cooking Time** 10 minutes	**Per Canapé** 19 calories, 1g fat (of which trace saturates), trace carbohydrate, 0.3g salt	Gluten free • Dairy free	**24**

2

Christmas Day

Freezing Tip

To freeze Complete the recipe, but only bake the rolls for 25 minutes, then cool, wrap and freeze for up to three months.
To use Bake from frozen in a preheated oven at 200°C (180°C fan oven) mark 6 for 12–15 minutes until golden and piping hot throughout.

Salt and Pepper Rolls

700g (1½lb) strong white bread flour, plus extra to dust

7g sachet fast-action dried yeast

1 tsp sea salt flakes, plus extra to sprinkle

1 tsp red peppercorns

1 tsp green peppercorns

2 tbsp olive oil, plus extra to grease

1 medium egg, beaten

1 Sift the flour into a large warmed bowl. Stir in the yeast. Crush the salt and peppercorns in a pestle and mortar and stir into the flour. Make a well in the centre of the flour, then pour in the oil and enough lukewarm water to make a soft dough, about 500ml (almost 1 pint). Knead for 5 minutes or until smooth. (Alternatively, put the flour, yeast, salt, peppercorns, oil and water in a freestanding mixer and knead to a soft dough with a dough hook.)

2 Transfer the dough to a large oiled bowl, cover with oiled clingfilm and leave in a warm place until doubled in size.

3 Turn the dough out on to a lightly floured worksurface and knead for about 5 minutes. Return the dough to the oiled bowl, cover with oiled clingfilm and leave in a warm place until doubled in size.

4 Punch the dough to knock back, then knead for 1 minute. Divide into 16 pieces and shape each one into a roll. Put the rolls on greased baking sheets, spaced well apart, cover with oiled clingfilm and leave for 30 minutes or until spongy. Preheat the oven to 220°C (200°C fan oven) mark 7.

5 Brush the rolls with beaten egg, sprinkle with a little salt and bake for 30–35 minutes until golden. Serve warm.

Makes	EASY		NUTRITIONAL INFORMATION	
16	**Preparation Time** 40 minutes, plus 2 hours rising	**Cooking Time** 30–35 minutes	**Per Roll** 157 calories, 2g fat (of which trace saturates), 33g carbohydrate, 0.3g salt	Vegetarian • Dairy free

Freezing Tip

To freeze Follow the recipe and cooking times in step 2, but don't glaze and bake for the final 5 minutes. Leave to cool in the tin. Wrap and freeze for up to two months.
To use Thaw, uncovered, at room temperature for 6 hours. Glaze the bread, put it on a hot baking sheet and bake at 220°C (200°C fan oven) mark 7 for 8–10 minutes or until hot throughout.

Walnut and Garlic Bread

oil to grease

500g (1lb 2oz) strong white bread flour with kibbled grains of rye and wheat, plus extra to dust

7g sachet fast-action dried yeast

2 tsp salt

1 tbsp malt extract

50g (2oz) butter, softened

3 garlic cloves, crushed

100g (3½oz) walnut pieces

For the glaze

1 tbsp milk mixed with 1 tbsp malt extract

1 Lightly grease a 20.5cm (8in) springform tin. Put the flour, yeast and salt in a freestanding mixer with a dough hook. Add 300ml (½ pint) lukewarm water and 1 tbsp malt extract, then mix to a pliable dough. Increase the speed and machine-knead for 5 minutes.

2 On a lightly floured worksurface, roll the dough into a rectangle about 40.5 x 28cm (16 x 11in). Mix together the butter and garlic, and spread over the dough. Scatter the walnuts over and, starting at one long edge, roll up the dough into a sausage. Cut into eight slices and put in the prepared tin. Cover with lightly oiled clingfilm and leave to rise in a warm place for 45 minutes or until doubled in size. Preheat the oven to 220°C (200°C fan oven) mark 7 and put a baking sheet in to heat. Remove the clingfilm, cover the bread with foil, and put on the hot baking sheet. Bake for 20 minutes. Reduce the oven temperature to 200°C (180°C fan oven) mark 6 and bake for 1 hour 10 minutes. Brush with the glaze and bake, uncovered, for a further 5 minutes or until golden brown. Leave in the tin to cool slightly. Serve warm.

EASY	NUTRITIONAL INFORMATION		Serves
Preparation Time 25 minutes, plus 45 minutes rising	**Cooking Time** about 1 hour 35 minutes	**Per Serving** 359 calories, 15g fat (of which 4g saturates), 52g carbohydrate, 1.3g salt	Vegetarian	**8**

Watercress Soup

250g (9oz) watercress, trimmed and coarse stalks removed

50g (2oz) butter

1 onion, finely chopped

700g (1½lb) potatoes, cut into small pieces

900ml (1½ pints) milk

900ml (1½ pints) vegetable stock

6 tbsp single cream

salt and ground black pepper

For the Parmesan crisps

125g (4oz) freshly grated Parmesan

½ tsp poppy seeds

1 To make the Parmesan crisps, preheat the oven to 200°C (180°C fan oven) mark 6 and line two baking sheets with baking parchment. Put heaped tablespoons of Parmesan on the sheets, spacing them well apart, and spread each one out slightly. Sprinkle with poppy seeds and bake for 5–10 minutes until lacy and golden. Leave on the baking sheet for 2–3 minutes to firm up slightly, then transfer to a wire rack to cool completely.

2 To make the soup, reserve a few sprigs of watercress to garnish, then roughly chop the rest. Melt the butter in a large pan, add the onion and cook gently for 8–10 minutes until soft. Add the potatoes and cook for 1 minute, then pour in the milk and stock and bring to the boil. Reduce the heat and simmer for 15–20 minutes until the potatoes are tender.

3 Take the pan off the heat. Stir in the chopped watercress, then transfer to a blender and blend, in batches, until smooth. Pour the soup into a clean pan, then add the cream and season with salt and pepper. Heat through, then serve garnished with the reserved watercress sprigs, with the Parmesan crisps on the side.

Cook's Tip

Watercress can wilt very quickly if you buy it in a bunch. To keep it fresh for a couple of days, store it in the refrigerator with the stems in a glass of water, and covered with a plastic bag.

Serves 6	EASY		NUTRITIONAL INFORMATION	
	Preparation Time 15 minutes	**Cooking Time** 30–40 minutes	**Per Serving** 324 calories, 18g fat (of which 10g saturates), 26g carbohydrate, 0.8g salt	Vegetarian • Gluten free

Try Something Different

Instead of salmon, use skinless rainbow trout fillet.
Replace the chives with fresh dill.

300g (11oz) skinless salmon fillet, roughly chopped

300g (11oz) ricotta or other soft cheese

juice of ½ large lemon

3 tbsp freshly chopped chives

2 large fennel bulbs, thinly sliced

2 large avocados, sliced

2 small courgettes, pared into strips with a vegetable peeler

10 tbsp vinaigrette dressing

125g (4oz) mixed salad leaves

8 slices toasted walnut bread

8 slices smoked salmon

salt and ground black pepper

lemon wedges to garnish

Quick Salmon Mousse

1   Put the salmon in a heatproof bowl and pour over enough boiling water to cover. Cover with clingfilm and leave to cool.

2   Drain the salmon and mash it into the cheese. Add the lemon juice and chives and season well with salt and pepper. Mix well, then cover and chill for up to one day.

3   Put the fennel, avocado and courgette in a shallow dish and spoon over the vinaigrette dressing.

4   Arrange the fennel, avocado and courgette on eight plates with the salad leaves. Put a slice of bread on each plate, then top with a mound of the salmon mixture and a fold of smoked salmon. Garnish with lemon wedges and serve immediately.

Serves 8	EASY	NUTRITIONAL INFORMATION
	Preparation Time 20 minutes, plus cooling	**Per Serving** 460 calories, 27g fat (of which 8g saturates), 18g carbohydrate, 3g salt

Red Onion and Gorgonzola Salad

1½ tbsp olive oil

4 red onions, about 500g (1lb 2oz) total weight, cut into wedges, keeping root intact

1 tbsp soft light brown sugar

2½ tbsp balsamic vinegar

350g (12oz) mixed salad leaves, washed and dried

275g (10oz) Gorgonzola cheese, crumbled

For the dressing

1 tbsp clear honey

1 tsp Dijon mustard

3 tbsp red wine vinegar

9 tbsp extra virgin olive oil

salt and ground black pepper

1 Heat the olive oil in a large frying pan. Add the onion wedges in a single layer, cover with a lid and cook over a low to moderate heat for 15 minutes or until the onions have softened and are beginning to brown on the underside.

2 Sprinkle the sugar over the onions, cover the pan and cook for a further 10 minutes until the exposed side starts to caramelise. Add the balsamic vinegar and cook uncovered until most of the vinegar has evaporated and the onions are sticky.

3 To make the dressing, put the honey, mustard, vinegar and oil in a bowl. Season to taste with salt and pepper and whisk together.

4 Put the salad leaves in a bowl with the onions and cheese and toss gently to mix. Divide among eight plates, then pour over the dressing and serve immediately.

EASY		NUTRITIONAL INFORMATION		Serves
Preparation Time 15 minutes	**Cooking Time** 30 minutes	**Per Serving** 284 calories, 24g fat (of which 9g saturates), 9g carbohydrate, 1.2g salt	Vegetarian • Gluten free	**8**

Cook's Tip

Chilli Mayonnaise: put 2 tbsp sweet chilli sauce, 1 tbsp freshly chopped coriander, grated zest and juice of 1 lime and 5 tbsp mayonnaise in a bowl and mix well. Season to taste with salt and pepper, cover and chill. This can be made a day ahead.

Chilli Crabcakes

vegetable oil to fry

3 spring onions, thinly sliced

2 garlic cloves, crushed

1 red chilli, seeded and chopped (see page 74)

350g (12oz) crabmeat

2 tsp tomato ketchup

4 tbsp mayonnaise

1 tsp Worcestershire sauce

175g (6oz) fresh white breadcrumbs

50g (2oz) plain flour

1 large egg, beaten

salt and ground black pepper

spring onion curls, sliced red chilli and lime wedges to garnish

Chilli Mayonnaise to serve (see Cook's Tip)

1 Heat 1 tbsp oil in a pan, add the spring onions and cook, stirring, for 3 minutes. Remove from the heat, stir in the garlic and chilli. Transfer the mixture to a bowl and leave to cool. Add the crabmeat, ketchup, mayonnaise, Worcestershire sauce and 50g (2oz) breadcrumbs and stir well. Season with salt and pepper. Using your hands, shape the mixture into 12 cakes. Put them on a baking sheet, cover and chill for at least 1 hour or overnight.

2 Season the flour with salt and pepper. Dip the cakes into the seasoned flour, then the beaten egg and the remaining breadcrumbs. Put the cakes back on the baking sheet and chill for a further 30 minutes.

3 Heat 2.5cm (1in) vegetable oil in a pan. Fry the cakes in batches for 2–3 minutes on each side until golden, then drain on kitchen paper. Season with salt and pepper, garnish with the spring onion curls, chilli and lime wedges, and serve with Chilli Mayonnaise.

Makes 12	EASY		NUTRITIONAL INFORMATION	
	Preparation Time 30 minutes, plus 1½ hours chilling	**Cooking Time** 15 minutes	**Per Crabcake** 206 calories, 12g fat (of which 2g saturates), 17g carbohydrate, 1.1g salt	Dairy free

8 large scallops or 16 small queen scallops with corals attached, about 300g (11oz) total weight

2 large ripe avocados

1 large garlic clove, crushed

6 small spring onions, finely chopped

1 green chilli, seeded and chopped (see page 74)

1½ tbsp grapeseed oil

grated zest and juice of 1 lime, plus extra to squeeze

8 large slices smoked salmon, about 400g (14oz) total weight and 23cm (9in) in length

salt and ground black pepper

rocket leaves and lime wedges to garnish

For the coriander dressing

25g (1oz) fresh coriander sprigs

1 small garlic clove, crushed

50ml (2fl oz) grapeseed oil

1 tbsp lime juice

Smoked Salmon Parcels

1 To make the coriander dressing, put all the ingredients in a blender and process until smooth.

2 To make the parcels, remove any tough membranes from the scallops and season with salt and pepper. Put them in a steamer and cook for about 5 minutes or until the flesh is just white. Alternatively, put the scallops on a heatproof plate, cover with another plate and steam over a pan of simmering water for about 3 minutes on each side. Drain and set on kitchen paper to cool.

3 Put the avocado, garlic, spring onions, chilli, oil and lime zest and juice in a bowl. Mash the avocado with a fork, mix well and season with salt and pepper.

4 Lay the salmon on a worksurface, put a large scallop or two small ones on each slice and spoon some avocado mixture on top. Roll the salmon around the filling. Put the parcels on serving plates and squeeze over a little lime juice. Drizzle with the coriander dressing and serve with rocket and lime wedges.

EASY	NUTRITIONAL INFORMATION		Serves
Preparation Time 35 minutes	**Cooking Time** 5–6 minutes	**Per Serving** 209 calories, 12g fat (of which 2g saturates), 3g carbohydrate, 2.3g salt	Gluten free • Dairy free	**8**

Lemon and Herb Roast Turkey

5.4–6.3kg (12–14lb) turkey, giblets removed for stock (see page 17)

½ quantity Chestnut and Butternut Squash Stuffing, thawed (see page 13)

125g (4oz) butter, softened

1 lemon, halved

3 fresh bay leaves

3 fresh sage leaves

2 fresh rosemary sprigs

8 rashers rindless streaky bacon

350g (12oz) chipolata sausages

salt and ground black pepper

a bunch of mixed herbs to garnish (optional)

Red Wine Gravy to serve (see page 14)

1 Take the turkey out of the refrigerator 45 minutes before stuffing it. Preheat the oven to 220°C (200°C fan oven) mark 7.

2 Put the turkey on a board and lift the neck flap. Use your fingers to ease the skin gently away from the turkey breast. Spoon in the stuffing, taking care not to overfill the cavity. Secure the flap with a cocktail stick.

3 Put a large sheet of foil in a flameproof roasting tin and put the turkey on top. Smear the turkey all over with butter, then squeeze over the lemon juice. Put the squeezed lemon halves and bay leaves inside the turkey, with a sage leaf and a sprig of rosemary, then snip over the remaining sage and rosemary. Season with salt and pepper.

4 Tie the turkey legs together with string. Bring the foil over the turkey and crimp the edges together, making sure there's plenty of space between the bird and the foil. Roast for 30 minutes, then reduce the oven temperature to 170°C (150°C fan oven) mark 3 and roast for a further 3½ hours.

5 Roll the rashers of bacon into neat rolls. Twist the chipolatas in two to make cocktail sausages and snip with scissors. Take the turkey out of the oven and increase the temperature to 200°C (180°C fan oven) mark 6. Pull off the foil and baste the turkey with the juices. Put the bacon rolls and chipolatas around the turkey, then roast for 40 minutes more, basting halfway through.

6 To check whether the turkey is cooked, pierce the thickest part of the flesh with a skewer; the juices should run clear. If there is any sign of blood, return the turkey to the oven for a further 10 minutes, then check again in the same way.

7 Tip the juices out of the turkey into the roasting tin, then lift the turkey, bacon and sausages on to a warm platter. Cover with foil and leave in a warm place for 30 minutes while you make the gravy. To garnish, stuff the turkey cavity with a bunch of mixed herbs.

EASY		NUTRITIONAL INFORMATION	Serves **8** with leftovers
Preparation Time 25 minutes	**Cooking Time** 4½–5 hours, plus 30 minutes resting	**Per Serving** 457 calories, 25g fat (of which 10g saturates), 2g carbohydrate, 1.2g salt	

Roast Goose with Wild Rice and Cranberry Stuffing

5kg (11lb) goose (with giblets for stock)

Wild Rice and Cranberry Stuffing, thawed (see page 13)

3 red-skinned apples

4 sprigs of fresh sage, plus extra to garnish

25g (1oz) butter

2 tbsp golden caster sugar

salt and ground black pepper

For the gravy

2 tbsp plain flour

150ml ($\frac{1}{4}$ pint) red wine

600ml (1 pint) Giblet Stock (see page 17)

2 tbsp redcurrant jelly

1 To make the goose easier to carve, remove the wishbone from the neck by lifting the flap and cutting around the bone with a small knife. Remove the wishbone. Using your fingers, ease the skin away from the flesh to make room for the stuffing, then put the goose on to a tray in the sink and pour a generous amount of freshly-boiled water over it. Pat it dry with kitchen paper.

2 Preheat the oven to 230°C (210°C fan oven) mark 8. Pack the neck of the goose with half of the stuffing and secure the neck shut with skewers or by using a trussing needle with fine string. Put any remaining stuffing on to a buttered sheet of foil and wrap it up.

Season the cavity of the bird with salt and pepper, then put in one whole apple and four sprigs of sage.

3 Put the goose on to a rack in a roasting tin and season well with salt and pepper. Roast for 30 minutes, basting occasionally, then remove and reserve any excess fat. Turn the oven down to 190°C (170°C fan oven) mark 5 and cook for a further 2$\frac{1}{2}$ hours, removing any excess fat every 20 minutes. Thirty minutes before the end of the cooking time, put the parcel of stuffing into the oven.

4 Test whether the goose is cooked by piercing the thigh with a thin skewer: the juices should run clear. Remove the goose from the oven and put it on a board. Cover with foil and leave to rest for at least 20 minutes.

5 Meanwhile, cut the remaining apples into thick wedges. Heat the butter in a heavy-based frying pan until it's no longer foaming. Add the apples and the sugar and stir-fry over a high heat for 4–5 minutes until caramelised, then put to one side.

6 To make the gravy, drain all but 3 tbsp fat from the roasting tin. Add the flour and stir to make a smooth paste. Add the wine and boil for 5 minutes, then add the stock and redcurrant jelly and mix well. Bring to the boil and simmer for 5 minutes. Strain before serving. Serve the goose, garnished with sage, with the stuffing and caramelised apples.

Serves	EASY		NUTRITIONAL INFORMATION
6	**Preparation Time** 45 minutes	**Cooking Time** about 3 hours, plus 20 minutes resting	**Per Serving** 820 calories, 51g fat (of which 18g saturates), 32g carbohydrate, 1.7g salt

Turkey Breast with Sausage, Cranberry and Apple Stuffing

turkey breast joint, about 1.4kg (3lb)

Sausage, Cranberry and Apple Stuffing, thawed (see page 12)

3 tbsp olive oil

1–2 tsp chicken seasoning

1 red eating apple

4–5 bay leaves

salt and ground black pepper

For the gravy

1 tbsp plain flour

2 tbsp cranberry jelly

300ml (½ pint) dry cider

600ml (1 pint) hot chicken stock

1 Preheat the oven to 200°C (180°C fan oven) mark 6. Put three or four wooden skewers in a bowl of water to soak.

2 Put the turkey joint on a board, skin side down, and cut down the middle, along the length of the joint, to just over three-quarters of the way through. Season with salt and pepper, spoon the stuffing inside, then push the joint back together. Secure with fine string and the soaked skewers. Weigh the joint, then calculate the cooking time: 20 minutes per 450g (1lb), plus 20 minutes extra. For the specified 1.4kg (3lb) turkey, the cooking time will be about 1 hour 20 minutes.

3 Put the joint in a roasting tin, skin side up, drizzle with olive oil and sprinkle with the chicken seasoning. Cover with foil and put in the oven.

4 Slice the apple into thin rounds. About 30 minutes before the end of the cooking time, remove the foil and push the apple slices and bay leaves under the string. Roast, uncovered, for the final 30 minutes or until cooked through – the juices should run clear when the thickest part of the meat is pierced with a skewer.

5 Transfer the turkey joint to a warm plate, cover with foil and leave to rest for about 20 minutes.

6 To make the gravy, drain off all but about 1 tbsp fat from the roasting tin. Add the flour and stir in. Put the roasting tin on the hob over a medium heat and cook for 1 minute, scraping the pan to mix in all the juices. Stir in the cranberry jelly and cider, bring to the boil and bubble until the liquid has reduced by half. Add the stock and cook for about 5 minutes until the gravy has thickened slightly. Remove the skewers from the turkey, cut the meat into slices and serve with the gravy.

EASY		NUTRITIONAL INFORMATION	Serves
Preparation Time 25 minutes	**Cooking Time** about 1 hour 20 minutes, plus 20 minutes resting	**Per Serving** 507 calories, 21g fat (of which 8g saturates), 12g carbohydrate, 1.2g salt	**8**

Cook's Tips

To prepare the duck The night before you want to serve this recipe, put the duck legs in a single layer in a plastic container and rub in 3 cloves crushed garlic, 2 tsp freshly chopped thyme and 1 tsp salt. Add 3 bay leaves, then cover and chill overnight. The next day, remove the duck from the refrigerator, rub off excess salt and rinse under cold running water. Pat dry with kitchen paper.

Make the red onion marmalade, cover and chill for up to three days. Reheat to serve.

Duck with Red Onion Marmalade

900ml (1½ pints) olive oil

4 duck legs with skin, marinated overnight (see Cook's Tips)

steamed cabbage and roast potato wedges to serve

For the red onion marmalade

125g (4oz) butter

550g (1¼lb) red onions, sliced

125g (4oz) kumquats, halved

125ml (4fl oz) sherry or wine vinegar

150g (5oz) golden caster sugar

grated zest and juice of 1 orange

300ml (½ pint) red wine

salt and ground black pepper

1 Preheat the oven to 170°C (150°C fan oven) mark 3. Heat the olive oil gently in a pan. Pack the prepared duck legs close together in a single layer in a baking dish and pour the oil over, covering the duck completely. Roast in the oven for 45 minutes until the duck is cooked through.

2 Meanwhile, to make the onion marmalade, melt the butter in a pan, add the onions, kumquats and vinegar and simmer, covered, for 15–20 minutes until the onions are soft, stirring every now and then. Add the sugar, turn up the heat and cook for 10 minutes, stirring, to caramelise the onions. Add the orange zest, juice and wine, then cook gently, uncovered, for 20 minutes until all the liquid has evaporated. Season with salt and pepper.

3 Lift the duck out of the oil and pat dry. Heat a large frying pan and cook the duck over a medium heat for 10–15 minutes until golden and crisp. Serve with the onion marmalade, cabbage and roast potato wedges.

Serves 4	EASY		NUTRITIONAL INFORMATION	
	Preparation Time 25 minutes, plus overnight marinating	**Cooking Time** about 1 hour	**Per Serving** 979 calories, 79g fat (of which 31g saturates), 53g carbohydrate, 0.7g salt	Gluten free

Get Ahead

To prepare ahead Complete the recipe to the end of step 1. Leave the tartlets to cool on a wire rack, then store in an airtight container for up to two days.
To use Complete the recipe.

Roasted Vegetable Tartlets

375g pack ready-rolled puff pastry, thawed if frozen
plain flour to dust
1 medium egg, beaten
2 tbsp coarse sea salt
300g (11oz) vegetable antipasti in olive oil
olive oil, if needed
2 tbsp balsamic vinegar
190g tub red pepper hummus
50g (2oz) wild rocket
salt and ground black pepper

1 Preheat the oven to 220°C (200°C fan oven) mark 7. Unroll the puff pastry on a lightly floured surface and cut it into six squares. Put the pastry squares on a large baking sheet and prick each one all over with a fork. Brush the surface with beaten egg and sprinkle the edges with sea salt. Bake for 5–7 minutes or until the pastry is golden brown and cooked through.

2 Pour 4 tbsp of olive oil from the jar of antipasti into a bowl (top it up with a little more olive oil if there's not enough in the antipasti jar). Add the balsamic vinegar, season with salt and pepper, mix well, then set aside.

3 To serve, divide the hummus among the six pastry bases and spread it over the surface. Put the bases on individual plates and spoon over the antipasti – there's no need to be neat. Whisk the balsamic vinegar dressing together. Add the rocket leaves and toss to coat, then pile a small handful of leaves on top of each tartlet. Serve immediately.

EASY		NUTRITIONAL INFORMATION		Makes
Preparation Time 15 minutes	**Cooking Time** about 7 minutes	**Per Tartlet** 356 calories, 24g fat (of which 1g saturates), 30g carbohydrate, 1.1g salt	Vegetarian	**6**

Nut and Cranberry Terrine

125g (4oz) long-grain rice

4 tbsp olive oil

1 onion, finely chopped

1 leek, trimmed and thinly sliced

4 celery sticks, thinly sliced

4 tbsp chopped mixed fresh herbs, such as sage, parsley and thyme

40g (1½oz) walnuts, toasted and roughly ground

125g (4oz) dolcelatte cheese, crumbled

1 large egg, beaten

40g (1½oz) fresh white breadcrumbs

125g (4oz) fromage frais or crème fraîche

Hot Water Crust Pastry (see Cook's Tip)

salt and ground black pepper

bay leaves to garnish

For the topping

125g (4oz) redcurrant jelly

1 tsp lemon juice

125g (4oz) cranberries or redcurrants, thawed if frozen

1 Cook the rice for 10 minutes or until just tender. Refresh under cold water, drain thoroughly and set aside. Heat the oil in a frying pan, add the onion, leek, celery and herbs and fry gently for 10 minutes until softened. Transfer to a bowl. Add the rice, walnuts, cheese, egg, breadcrumbs and fromage frais or crème fraîche. Season well and stir until combined.

2 Preheat the oven to 220°C (200°C fan oven) mark 7. Roll out the pastry to a 25.5 x 20.5cm (10 x 8in) rectangle and use to line a 900g (2lb) loaf tin, pressing the dough into the corners. Trim the overhanging pastry and reserve.

3 Spoon the rice mixture into the pastry case and smooth the surface. Divide the pastry trimmings in half, roll each piece into a long thin rope and twist the two ropes together. Dampen the pastry edges and top with the pastry twist, pressing down gently. Cook the terrine in the oven for 45–50 minutes until golden and a skewer inserted into the centre comes out hot. Remove from the oven and leave to cool.

4 To make the topping, heat the redcurrant jelly in a small pan with the lemon juice and 1 tbsp water until melted, then simmer for 3 minutes. Remove from the heat and stir in the fruit.

5 To unmould the pie, turn the loaf tin upside-down and tap gently. Spoon the topping over and leave to set. When cold, garnish with bay leaves.

Cook's Tip

Hot Water Crust Pastry: sift 225g (8oz) plain flour and a pinch of salt into a bowl and make a well in the middle. Heat 50g (2oz) white vegetable fat and 100ml (3½fl oz) water in a pan until it comes to the boil. Pour into the flour and work together, using a wooden spoon. When cool enough to handle, knead lightly until smooth; use while still warm and pliable.

A LITTLE EFFORT		NUTRITIONAL INFORMATION		Serves
Preparation Time 45 minutes, plus cooling	**Cooking Time** 1 hour 10 minutes	**Per Serving** 495 calories, 28g fat (of which 12g saturates), 52g carbohydrate, 0.7g salt	Vegetarian	**8**

Get Ahead

To prepare ahead Make both stuffings and the sauce (step 4), then cover and chill for up to two days.
To use Bring the stuffings up to room temperature, gently reheat the sauce, and complete the recipe.

Mushroom and Aubergine Tian

1 medium aubergine, thinly sliced

1 medium courgette, thinly sliced

3 tbsp olive oil

4 portabella or large flat mushrooms, stalks trimmed off

½ quantity Fennel and Pinenut Stuffing (see page 13)

1 small red onion, cut into thin wedges

150ml (¼ pint) port

225ml (8fl oz) vegetable stock

100g (3½oz) redcurrant jelly

3 strips orange zest

juice of ½ lemon

salt and ground black pepper

For the mushroom and chestnut stuffing

15g (½oz) butter

15g (½oz) dark muscovado sugar

1 onion, finely chopped

1½ tbsp balsamic vinegar

1 small celery stick, chopped

2 tbsp freshly chopped oregano

4 tbsp dried cranberries

40g (1½oz) fresh breadcrumbs

75g (3oz) vacuum-packed cooked chestnuts, chopped

100g (3½oz) chestnut mushrooms, chopped

1 To make the mushroom and chestnut stuffing, heat the butter and sugar in a pan. Add the onion and cook for 5 minutes until soft. Add the vinegar and celery, bring to the boil and cook for 1 minute. Leave to cool. Add the oregano, cranberries, breadcrumbs, chestnuts and mushrooms. Season with salt and pepper and mix well.

2 Brush the aubergine and courgette with 2 tbsp olive oil. Heat a large non-stick frying pan and fry the vegetables, in batches, for about 2 minutes on each side, until pale golden.

3 Preheat the oven to 200°C (180°C fan oven) mark 6. Lay the aubergine slices overlapping on top of each flat mushroom. Divide the fennel stuffing among the mushrooms and season with salt and pepper. Top with some mushroom and chestnut stuffing and season again. Arrange courgette slices over the stuffing, overlapping them, then top with onion wedges. Carefully put the mushrooms in an ovenproof dish, drizzle the remaining oil over and bake for 30 minutes, until golden.

4 Meanwhile, put the port, stock, redcurrant jelly, orange zest and lemon juice in a wide pan. Bring to the boil and bubble for 10 minutes until reduced and syrupy. Taste and season if necessary; discard the orange zest. Divide the mushrooms among four warmed plates, drizzle with the sauce and serve.

Serves 4	A LITTLE EFFORT		NUTRITIONAL INFORMATION	
	Preparation Time 40 minutes	**Cooking Time** about 50 minutes	**Per Serving** 588 calories, 28g fat (of which 10g saturates), 63g carbohydrate, 1.1g salt	Vegetarian

Freezing Tip

To freeze Complete the recipe to the end of step 2, then cool, seal in large freezer bags and freeze for up to one month.
To use Cook from frozen, allowing an additional 15–20 minutes total cooking time.

Crispy Roast Potatoes

1.8kg (4lb) potatoes, preferably King Edward, cut into two-bite pieces

2 tsp paprika

2–3 tbsp goose or white vegetable fat

salt

1 Put the potatoes in a pan of salted cold water. Cover and bring to the boil. Boil for 7 minutes, then drain well in a colander.

2 Sprinkle the paprika over the potatoes in the colander, then cover and shake the potatoes roughly, so they become fluffy around the edges.

3 Preheat the oven to 220°C (200°C fan oven) mark 7. Heat the fat in a large roasting tin on the hob. When it sizzles, add the potatoes. Tilt the pan to coat, taking care as the fat will splutter. Roast in the oven for 1 hour.

4 Reduce the oven temperature to 200°C (180°C fan oven) mark 6 and roast for a further 40 minutes. Shake the potatoes only once or twice during cooking, otherwise the edges won't crisp and brown. Season with a little salt before serving.

Serves 8	EASY		NUTRITIONAL INFORMATION	
	Preparation Time 20 minutes	**Cooking Time** 1 hour 50 minutes	**Per Serving** 211 calories, 6g fat (of which 3g saturates), 37g carbohydrate, 0.1g salt	Gluten free • Dairy free

Freezing Tip

To freeze Omit step 1 of the recipe. Complete step 2, then cool, add the chestnuts, wrap and freeze.
To use Thaw for 1 hour. Complete step 1 of the recipe. Stir-fry the chestnut mixture for 1 minute, then add the Brussels sprouts and complete the recipe.

Brussels Sprouts with Pancetta

900g (2lb) Brussels sprouts, halved
1 tbsp olive oil
130g pack pancetta cubes
2 shallots, chopped
250g (9oz) peeled and cooked (or vacuum-packed) chestnuts
15g (½oz) butter
a pinch of freshly grated nutmeg
salt

1 Bring a pan of salted water to the boil, add the Brussels sprouts and blanch for 2 minutes. Drain and briefly refresh under cold water. Drain well.

2 Heat the oil in a pan and fry the pancetta for 3–4 minutes until golden. Add the shallots and stir-fry for about 5 minutes until softened.

3 Add the Brussels sprouts and chestnuts to the pan and stir-fry for another 5 minutes until heated through.

4 Add the butter and nutmeg and toss well. Serve immediately.

EASY		NUTRITIONAL INFORMATION		Serves
Preparation Time 5 minutes	**Cooking Time** 15 minutes	**Per Serving** 174 calories, 9g fat (of which 3g saturates), 17g carbohydrate, 0.6g salt	Gluten free	**8**

Spinach with Tomatoes

50g (2oz) butter
2 garlic cloves, crushed
450g (1lb) baby plum tomatoes, halved
250g (9oz) baby spinach leaves
a large pinch of freshly grated nutmeg
salt and ground black pepper

1 Heat half the butter in a pan, add the garlic and cook until just soft. Add the tomatoes and cook for 4–5 minutes until just beginning to soften.

2 Put the spinach and a little water in a clean pan, cover and cook for 2–3 minutes until just wilted. Drain well, chop roughly and stir into the tomatoes.

3 Add the remaining butter and heat through gently. Season well with salt and pepper, stir in the nutmeg and serve.

Serves 6	EASY		NUTRITIONAL INFORMATION	
	Preparation Time 10 minutes	Cooking Time 15 minutes	Per Serving 85 calories, 7g fat (of which 5g saturates), 3g carbohydrate, 0.3g salt	Vegetarian • Gluten free

Freezing Tip

To freeze Cook the carrots for only 5 minutes, then cool and freeze with the remaining liquid.
To use Thaw for 5 hours, then reheat in a pan for 5–6 minutes or cook on full power in a 900W microwave for 7–8 minutes.

Lemon and Orange Carrots

900g (2lb) carrots, cut into long batons

150ml (¼ pint) orange juice

juice of 2 lemons

150ml (¼ pint) dry white wine

50g (2oz) butter

3 tbsp light muscovado sugar

4 tbsp freshly chopped coriander to garnish

1 Put the carrots, orange and lemon juices, wine, butter and sugar in a pan. Cover and bring to the boil.

2 Remove the lid and cook until almost all the liquid has evaporated, about 10 minutes. Serve sprinkled with the coriander.

EASY		NUTRITIONAL INFORMATION		Serves
Preparation Time 10 minutes	**Cooking Time** 10–15 minutes	**Per Serving** 127 calories, 6g fat (of which 3g saturates), 17g carbohydrate, 0.2g salt	Vegetarian • Gluten free	**8**

Get Ahead

Red cabbage improves if made a day ahead. Complete step 1, cover and chill.
To use Reheat the cabbage gently, add the pears and complete the recipe.

1 tbsp olive oil

1 red onion, halved and sliced

2 garlic cloves, crushed

1 large red cabbage, about 1kg (2¼lb), shredded

2 tbsp light muscovado sugar

2 tbsp red wine vinegar

8 juniper berries

¼ tsp ground allspice

300ml (½ pint) vegetable stock

2 pears, cored and sliced

salt and ground black pepper

fresh thyme sprigs to garnish

Braised Red Cabbage

1 Heat the oil in a large pan, add the onion and fry for 5 minutes. Add the remaining ingredients, except the pears, and season with salt and pepper. Bring to the boil, then cover and simmer for 30 minutes.

2 Add the pears and cook for a further 15 minutes or until nearly all the liquid has evaporated and the cabbage is tender. Serve hot, garnished with thyme.

Serves	EASY		NUTRITIONAL INFORMATION	
6	**Preparation Time** 15 minutes	**Cooking Time** about 50 minutes	**Per Serving** 63 calories, 1g fat (of which 0g saturates), 12g carbohydrate, 0.9g salt	Vegetarian Gluten free • Dairy free

Freezing Tip

To freeze Complete the recipe, then cool, wrap and freeze for up to one month.

To use Thaw overnight at room temperature, then reheat at 200°C (180°C fan oven) mark 6 for 20 minutes in an ovenproof dish with 200ml (7fl oz) hot stock.

Spicy Roasted Roots

3 carrots, sliced lengthways

3 parsnips, sliced lengthways

3 tbsp olive oil

1 butternut squash, chopped

2 red onions, cut into wedges

2 leeks, sliced

3 garlic cloves, roughly chopped

2 tbsp mild curry paste

salt and ground black pepper

1. Preheat the oven to 200°C (180°C fan oven) mark 6. Put the carrots and parsnips in a large roasting tin, drizzle with 1 tbsp oil and cook for 40 minutes.

2. Add the butternut squash, onions, leeks and garlic to the roasting tin. Season with salt and pepper, then drizzle over the remaining 2 tbsp oil.

3. Roast for 45 minutes until the vegetables are tender and golden. Stir in the curry paste and return to the oven for a further 10 minutes. Serve immediately.

EASY		NUTRITIONAL INFORMATION		Serves
Preparation Time 25 minutes	**Cooking Time** about 1½ hours	**Per Serving** 134 calories, 8g fat (of which 1g saturates), 14g carbohydrate, 0.1g salt	Vegetarian Gluten free • Dairy free	**8**

3

Festive Entertaining

Salmon and Asparagus Terrine

75g (3oz) butter, plus extra to grease

1 garlic clove, chopped

1 medium red chilli, seeded and finely chopped (see Cook's Tips)

½ lemongrass stalk, finely chopped

250g (9oz) asparagus spears

250g (9oz) sliced smoked salmon

3 tbsp freshly chopped dill, plus extra sprigs to garnish

1kg (2¼lb) salmon fillet, skinned and boned

salt and ground black pepper

1 Put the butter in a pan and melt over a low heat. Bring to the boil and skim off any impurities until clear. Pour into a bowl and add the garlic, chilli and lemongrass. Leave to infuse.

2 Cook the asparagus in a pan of salted boiling water for 2–3 minutes until just tender. Drain and refresh under cold water. Drain well.

3 Grease and line a 900g (2lb) loaf tin with foil, then grease the foil. Line the bottom and sides of the tin with smoked salmon, reserving some for the top. Sprinkle over 1 tbsp chopped dill, drizzle with a little of the infused butter and season with salt and pepper.

4 Preheat the oven to 180°C (160°C fan oven) mark 4. Cut the salmon fillet in half lengthways to fit it in the loaf tin and put one of the pieces inside. Sprinkle over 1 tbsp of the chopped dill and drizzle with a little of the infused butter. Layer up the terrine with the asparagus spears and the other salmon half, sprinkling the remaining dill, infused butter and salt and pepper on top of the salmon. Finish with a layer of smoked salmon, then cover with foil.

5 Put the loaf tin in a roasting tin and half-fill the roasting tin with hot water. Cook the terrine in the preheated oven for 50 minutes–1 hour or until a skewer inserted in the middle for 30 seconds comes out warm. Leave to cool, then weigh the terrine down with two food cans and chill overnight. To serve, turn out the terrine, decorate with dill sprigs and slice.

Cook's Tips

Chillies vary enormously in strength, from quite mild to blisteringly hot, depending on the type of chilli and its ripeness. Taste a small piece first to check it's not too hot for you.

Be extremely careful when handling chillies not to touch or rub your eyes with your fingers, as they will sting. Wash knives immediately after handling chillies for the same reason. As a precaution, use rubber gloves when preparing them if you like.

Serves 10	EASY		NUTRITIONAL INFORMATION	
	Preparation Time 40 minutes, plus overnight chilling	**Cooking Time** about 1 hour	**Per Serving** 278 calories, 18g fat (of which 6g saturates), 1g carbohydrate, 1.4g salt	Gluten free

Cook's Tips

There'll be a lot of hot liquid in the parcel of salmon, so ask someone to help you lift it out of the oven.

To check the fish is cooked, ease a knife into one of the slashes in the skin. The flesh should look opaque and the knife should come out hot.

To prepare ahead Complete the recipe to the end of step 3, then keep the salmon wrapped and chilled for up to one day.

Roasted Salmon

3 lemons, 2 sliced and the juice of ½, plus extra lemon slices to garnish

2 salmon sides, filleted, each 1.4kg (3lb), skin on, boned and trimmed

2 tbsp dry white wine

salt and ground black pepper

cucumber slices and 2 large bunches of watercress to garnish

For the dressing

500g carton crème fraîche

500g carton natural yogurt

2 tbsp horseradish sauce

3 tbsp freshly chopped tarragon

4 tbsp capers, roughly chopped, plus extra to garnish

¼ cucumber, seeded and finely chopped

1 Preheat the oven to 190°C (170°C fan oven) mark 5. Take two pieces of foil, each large enough to wrap one side of salmon, and put a piece of greaseproof paper on top. Divide the lemon slices between each piece of greaseproof paper and lay the salmon on top, skin side up. Season with salt and pepper, then pour over the lemon juice and wine.

2 Score the skin of each salmon fillet at 4cm (1½in) intervals to mark 10 portions. Scrunch the foil around each fillet, keeping it loose so the fish doesn't stick. Cook for 25 minutes until the flesh is just opaque. Unwrap the foil and cook for a further 5 minutes until the skin is crisp. Leave the fish to cool quickly in a cold place. Re-wrap and chill.

3 Put all the dressing ingredients in a bowl and season with salt and pepper. Mix well, then cover and chill.

4 Serve the salmon on a platter garnished with lemon, cucumber and watercress. Garnish the dressing with capers and chopped cucumber.

Serves 20	EASY		NUTRITIONAL INFORMATION	
	Preparation Time 20 minutes, plus cooling and chilling	**Cooking Time** about 30 minutes	**Per Serving** 347 calories, 25g fat (of which 9g saturates), 3g carbohydrate, 0.2g salt	Gluten free

Try Something Different

Instead of salmon, use smoked haddock fillet, poached for 5 minutes, then drained, skinned and flaked into chunky pieces.

Spinach and Smoked Salmon Tart

225g (8oz) plain flour, plus extra to dust

75g (3oz) butter, cubed

a pinch of salt

125g (4oz) fresh spinach leaves

200g (7oz) crème fraîche

2 medium eggs, beaten

100g (3½oz) smoked salmon, trimmed into thin strips

25g (1oz) freshly grated Parmesan

salt and ground black pepper

1 Put the flour, butter and salt in a food processor. Whiz briefly until the mixture resembles fine breadcrumbs. Add 3–4 tbsp cold water and whiz briefly to form a soft dough. Roll out the dough on a floured worksurface until it's large enough to line a 23cm (9in) fluted flan tin. Press the pastry into the tin and trim the edges with a sharp knife. Prick the base a few times with a fork and chill the pastry case for 30 minutes. Preheat the oven to 200°C (180°C fan oven) mark 6. Put a baking sheet in the oven. Bake the pastry blind (see Glossary) for 10 minutes, then bake for a further 10–15 minutes until golden.

2 Put the spinach leaves in a pan, add a little boiling water and cook for 1 minute until wilted. Refresh under cold water and drain well. Put the spinach in a large bowl and add the crème fraîche, eggs and smoked salmon. Season with salt and pepper and stir well. Spoon the mixture into the pastry case. Sprinkle the Parmesan over the top of the tart and bake for 25 minutes until set and golden. Serve hot or at room temperature.

EASY	NUTRITIONAL INFORMATION	Serves
Preparation Time 25 minutes, plus 30 minutes chilling **Cooking Time** about 50 minutes	**Per Serving** 629 calories, 42g fat (of which 26g saturates), 46g carbohydrate, 1.9g salt	4

Cook's Tip

Blue Cheese Sauce: melt 50g (2oz) butter in a small pan. Add 3 tbsp plain flour and cook, stirring, for 1 minute. Remove from the heat and gradually stir in 350ml (12fl oz) milk. (Alternatively, use 300ml (½ pint) milk and the reserved fish poaching liquid.) Return the pan to a gentle heat and cook the sauce, stirring, until thickened and smooth. Crumble in 125g (4oz) Stilton cheese, then add 4 tbsp single cream and season with salt and pepper.

Seafood Pie with Blue Cheese

450g (1lb) cod, haddock or whiting fillet

50ml (2fl oz) milk

25g (1oz) butter, plus extra to grease

350g (12oz) leeks, sliced

freshly grated nutmeg

225g (8oz) large raw peeled prawns

Blue Cheese Sauce (see Cook's Tip)

700g (1½lb) floury potatoes, cut into 5mm (¼in) slices, boiled for 5 minutes, then drained

salt and ground black pepper

1   Put the fish in a shallow pan and pour over the milk. Season lightly with salt and pepper, cover and poach for about 5 minutes or until the fish flakes easily. Drain, reserving the cooking liquid. Flake the fish, discarding the skin and bones. Set aside.

2   Melt the butter in a pan and fry the leeks for 3 minutes, adding plenty of nutmeg. Lightly butter a 1.7 litre (3 pint) pie dish. Preheat the oven to 190°C (170°C fan oven) mark 5.

3   Mix the fish, leeks and prawns together in the prepared pie dish. Spoon half of the cheese sauce over the top. Layer the cooked potato slices over the filling, then pour the remaining sauce over the potatoes. Place the dish on a baking sheet and bake for 45 minutes or until the pie is bubbling and golden.

Serves 4	EASY		NUTRITIONAL INFORMATION
	Preparation Time 40 minutes	**Cooking Time** about 1 hour	**Per Serving** 634 calories, 32g fat (of which 20g saturates), 42g carbohydrate, 1.5g salt

Ginger and Honey-glazed Ham

4.5–6.8kg (10–15lb) unsmoked gammon on the bone

2 shallots, halved

6 cloves

3 bay leaves

2 celery sticks, cut into 5cm (2in) pieces

2 tbsp English mustard

5cm (2in) piece fresh root ginger, peeled and thinly sliced

225g (8oz) dark brown sugar

2 tbsp clear honey

8 tbsp brandy or Madeira

For the chutney

4 mangoes, chopped into 5cm (2in) chunks

1 tsp mixed spice

4 cardamom pods, seeds removed and crushed

½ tsp ground cinnamon

4 tbsp raisins

1 Put the gammon in a large pan. Add the shallots, cloves, bay leaves, celery and cold water to cover. Bring to the boil, cover and simmer gently for about 5 hours. Remove any scum with a slotted spoon. Lift the ham out of the pan, discard the vegetables and herbs, and leave to cool.

2 Preheat the oven to 200°C (180°C fan oven) mark 6. Using a sharp knife, cut away the skin to leave a layer of fat. Score a diamond pattern in the fat and put the ham in a roasting tin. Spread with the mustard and tuck the ginger into the fat. Put the sugar, honey and brandy or Madeira in a pan and heat gently until the sugar has dissolved. Brush over the ham.

3 Put the chutney ingredients in a bowl, add any remaining glaze and mix well. Spoon the mixture around the ham. Cook the ham for 30–40 minutes, basting every 10 minutes. Remove the ham from the tin and set aside. Stir the chutney and put it under a preheated grill for 5 minutes to caramelise the mango. Transfer to a dish and serve with the ham.

EASY	NUTRITIONAL INFORMATION		Serves
Preparation Time 45 minutes, plus cooling	**Cooking Time** about 5¾ hours	**Per Serving** 440 calories, 15g fat (of which 5g saturates), 38g carbohydrate, 4.4g salt	Gluten free • Dairy free	**10**

Cook's Tip

Red Wine Sauce: soften 350g (12oz) shallots, finely chopped, in 2 tbsp olive oil for 5 minutes. Add 3 garlic cloves, chopped, and 3 tbsp tomato purée, cook for 1 minute, then add 2 tbsp balsamic vinegar. Simmer briskly until reduced to almost nothing, then add 200ml (7fl oz) red wine and reduce by half. Pour in 600ml (1 pint) beef stock and simmer until reduced by one-third.

Fillet of Beef en Croûte

1–1.4kg (2¼–3lb) trimmed fillet of beef

50g (2oz) butter

2 shallots, chopped

15g (½oz) dried porcini mushrooms, soaked in 100ml (3½fl oz) boiling water

2 garlic cloves, chopped

225g (8oz) flat mushrooms, finely chopped

2 tsp chopped fresh thyme, plus extra sprigs to garnish

175g (6oz) chicken liver pâté

175g (6oz) thinly sliced Parma ham

375g ready-rolled puff pastry

1 medium egg, beaten

salt and ground black pepper

Red Wine Sauce (see Cook's Tip) to serve

1 Season the beef with salt and pepper. Melt 25g (1oz) butter in a large frying pan and, when foaming, add the beef and brown it all over for 4–5 minutes. Transfer to a plate and leave to cool.

2 Melt the remaining butter in a pan, add the shallots and cook for 1 minute. Drain the porcini mushrooms, reserving the liquid, and chop them. Add them to the pan with the garlic, the reserved liquid and the fresh mushrooms. Turn up the heat and cook until the liquid has evaporated, then season with salt and pepper and add the thyme. Leave to cool.

3 Put the chicken liver pâté in a bowl and beat until smooth. Add the mushroom mixture and stir well. Spread half the mushroom mixture evenly over one side of the fillet. Lay half the Parma ham on a length of clingfilm, overlapping the slices. Invert the mushroom-topped beef on to the ham. Spread the remaining mushroom mixture on the other side of the beef, then lay the rest of the Parma ham, also overlapping, on top of the mushroom mixture. Wrap the beef in the clingfilm to form a firm sausage shape, and chill for 30 minutes. Preheat the oven to 220°C (200°C fan oven) mark 7.

4 On a lightly floured surface, cut off one-third of the pastry. Roll out to 3mm (⅛in) thick and 2.5cm (1in) larger all round than the beef. Prick all over with a fork. Transfer to a baking sheet and bake for 12–15 minutes until brown and crisp. Leave to cool, then trim to the size of the beef. Remove the clingfilm from the beef, brush with the egg and place it on the cooked pastry.

5 Roll out the remaining pastry to a 25.5 x 30.5cm (10 x 12in) rectangle. Roll over a lattice pastry cutter and gently ease the lattice open. Cover the beef with the lattice, tuck the ends under and seal the edges. Brush with the beaten egg, then cook on a baking sheet for 40 minutes for rare, 45 minutes for medium. Leave to stand for 10 minutes before carving. Garnish with thyme and serve with Red Wine Sauce.

FOR THE CONFIDENT COOK		NUTRITIONAL INFORMATION	Serves
Preparation Time 1 hour, plus soaking and chilling	**Cooking Time** about 1 hour 20 minutes, plus standing	**Per Serving** 802 calories, 53g fat (of which 15g saturates), 27g carbohydrate, 2.4g salt	**6**

Get Ahead

This roast is ideal to serve for a special occasion, as nearly all the work is done in advance, leaving you free to chat to your guests.

Spiced Leg of Lamb

1.8kg (4lb) leg of lamb
2 tbsp each cumin seeds and coriander seeds
50g (2oz) blanched or flaked almonds
1 medium onion, roughly chopped
6 garlic cloves, roughly chopped
2.5cm (1in) piece fresh root ginger, peeled and grated
4 hot green chillies, seeded and roughly chopped (see page 74)
500g carton natural yogurt
$1/2$ tsp each cayenne pepper and garam masala
$31/2$ tsp salt
4 tbsp vegetable oil
$1/2$ tsp whole cloves
16 cardamom pods
1 cinnamon stick
10 black peppercorns
fresh flat-leafed parsley sprigs to garnish

1 Trim off and discard all the fat and parchment-like white skin from the lamb. Put the meat in a large, shallow ceramic dish and set aside. Put the cumin and coriander seeds in a pan and cook briefly over a high heat until they begin to release their aromas. Transfer the seeds to a mortar and grind to a fine powder with a pestle. Set aside.

2 Put the almonds, onion, garlic, ginger, chillies and 3 tbsp of the yogurt in a food processor and blend to a paste. Put the remaining yogurt in a bowl, stir well and add the paste, cayenne pepper, garam masala and salt. Stir well, then add the ground cumin and coriander and stir well to mix.

3 Spoon the yogurt mixture over the lamb and use a pastry brush to spread it evenly. Turn the lamb over, making sure it is well coated. Cover with clingfilm and leave to marinate in the refrigerator for 24 hours.

4 Remove the lamb from the refrigerator about 45 minutes before you want to cook it to allow it to reach room temperature. Preheat the oven to 200°C (180°C fan oven) mark 6. Put the lamb and marinade in a roasting tin. Heat the oil in a small frying pan, add the cloves, cardamom pods, cinnamon and peppercorns, and fry until they begin to release their aromas. Pour the spices over the lamb.

5 Cover the lamb and roasting tin with foil and roast for $1/2$ hours. Remove the foil and roast for a further 45 minutes, basting occasionally. Put the lamb on a serving dish; pick out the spices and set aside to garnish. Press the sauce through a fine sieve into a bowl. Garnish the lamb with the flat-leafed parsley and the reserved spices and serve with the sauce on the side.

Serves	EASY		NUTRITIONAL INFORMATION	
6	**Preparation Time** 25 minutes, plus 24 hours marinating	**Cooking Time** 2¼ hours	**Per Serving** 671 calories, 47g fat (of which 13g saturates), 11g carbohydrate, 2.2g salt	Gluten free

Marinated Duck with Prunes

4 duck breasts

8 ready-to-eat pitted prunes

8 large garlic cloves, boiled for 10 minutes, then peeled

25g (1oz) butter

1 tsp plain flour

Braised Red Cabbage (see page 70) and mashed potato to serve

For the marinade

250ml (9fl oz) prune juice

1 carrot and 2 shallots, finely chopped

1 bay leaf and 1 fresh parsley sprig

1 fresh thyme sprig, plus extra to garnish

1 tsp black peppercorns

125ml (4fl oz) red wine

4 tbsp brandy

4 tbsp olive oil

½ tsp salt

1 To make the marinade, set aside half the prune juice, then mix all the remaining ingredients in a dish large enough to hold the duck in a single layer. Add the duck, cover and chill overnight, turning occasionally.

2 Soak four small wooden skewers in water. Remove the duck from the marinade and pat it dry on kitchen paper. Transfer the marinade to a pan, bring to the boil; simmer until reduced by half. Strain and keep warm. Push the prunes and garlic on to the skewers.

3 Melt the butter in a large frying pan, add the duck, skin side down, and fry for 8 minutes or until golden. Turn and cook for 3–4 minutes. Remove from the pan and leave to rest for 10 minutes. Cook the prune skewers in the same pan, turning, until the garlic colours. Remove and set aside. Add the flour to the pan and cook, stirring, for 2–3 seconds. Add the marinade and remaining prune juice and simmer, stirring, until thickened and glossy. Serve on warmed plates with the red cabbage and mashed potato. Garnish with thyme.

Serves	EASY		NUTRITIONAL INFORMATION
4	**Preparation Time** 30 minutes, plus overnight marinating	**Cooking Time** about 45 minutes, plus resting	**Per Serving** 654 calories, 51g fat (of which 14g saturates), 38g carbohydrate, 0.6g salt

Freezing Tip

To freeze Complete the recipe to the end of step 3, then cool and freeze for up to one week.
To use Thaw overnight in the refrigerator and complete the recipe.

Roasted Stuffed Peppers

40g (1½oz) butter

4 red peppers, halved and seeded, leaving the stalks intact

3 tbsp olive oil

350g (12oz) chestnut mushrooms, roughly chopped

4 tbsp freshly chopped chives

100g (3½oz) feta cheese

50g (2oz) fresh white breadcrumbs

25g (1oz) freshly grated Parmesan

salt and ground black pepper

1 Preheat the oven to 180°C (160°C fan oven) mark 4. Use a little of the butter to grease a shallow ovenproof dish, then put in the peppers side by side, hollow side up.

2 Heat the remaining butter and 1 tbsp of the oil in a pan. Add the mushrooms and fry until they are golden and there's no excess liquid left in the pan. Stir in the chives, then spoon the mixture into the pepper halves.

3 Crumble the feta cheese over the mushrooms. Mix the breadcrumbs and Parmesan in a bowl, then sprinkle the mixture over the top.

4 Season with salt and pepper and drizzle with the remaining oil. Roast for 45 minutes or until golden and tender. Serve warm.

EASY		NUTRITIONAL INFORMATION		Serves
Preparation Time 20 minutes	**Cooking Time** about 50 minutes	**Per Serving** 375 calories, 25g fat (of which 11g saturates), 27g carbohydrate, 1.5g salt	Vegetarian	**4**

Artichoke and Mushroom Lasagne

3 tbsp olive oil

225g (8oz) onions, roughly chopped

3 garlic cloves, crushed

25g (1oz) walnuts

1.1kg (2½lb) mixed mushrooms, such as brown-cap and button, roughly chopped

125g (4oz) cherry tomatoes

50g (2oz) butter, plus extra to grease

50g (2oz) plain flour

1.1 litres (2 pints) whole milk

2 bay leaves

2 tbsp lemon juice

200g pack fresh chilled lasagne

400g can artichoke hearts in water, drained and halved

75g (3oz) freshly grated Parmesan

salt and ground black pepper

fresh oregano sprigs to garnish (optional)

1 Heat the oil in a large pan and fry the onions gently for 10 minutes until soft. Add the garlic and walnuts and fry for 3–4 minutes, until pale golden. Stir in the mushrooms and cook for 10 minutes. Let the mixture bubble briskly for a further 10 minutes or until all the liquid has evaporated. Add the tomatoes to the pan, then remove from the heat and set aside.

2 Preheat the oven to 200°C (180°C fan oven) mark 6. Melt the butter in a pan, add the flour and stir over a gentle heat for 1 minute. Slowly whisk in the milk until you have a smooth mixture. Bring to the boil, add the bay leaves, then stir over a gentle heat for 10 minutes until thickened and smooth. Add the lemon juice and season to taste with salt and pepper. Discard the bay leaves.

3 Grease a shallow ovenproof dish and layer lasagne sheets over the base. Spoon half the mushroom mixture over, then half the artichokes. Cover with a layer of lasagne and half the sauce. Spoon the remaining mushroom mixture over, then the remaining artichokes. Top with the remaining lasagne sheets. Stir the Parmesan into the remaining sauce and spoon evenly over the top of the lasagne.

4 Cook in the oven for 40–50 minutes until golden and bubbling. Garnish with oregano sprigs if using, and serve.

Get Ahead

To prepare ahead Complete the recipe to the end of step 3, then cool, cover and chill for up to three hours.
To use Remove from the refrigerator about 30 minutes before cooking, then complete the recipe.

EASY		NUTRITIONAL INFORMATION		Serves
Preparation Time 25 minutes	**Cooking Time** about 1½ hours	**Per Serving** 322 calories, 21g fat (of which 11g saturates), 19g carbohydrate, 0.7g salt	Vegetarian	**6**

Chilli Onions with Goat's Cheese

75g (3oz) unsalted butter, softened

2 medium red chillies, seeded and finely chopped (see page 74)

1 tsp crushed dried chillies

6 small red onions

3 x 100g (3½oz) goat's cheese logs, with rind

salt and ground black pepper

balsamic vinegar to serve

1   Preheat the oven to 200°C (180°C fan oven) mark 6. Put the butter in a small bowl, beat in the fresh and dried chillies and season well with salt and pepper.

2   Cut off the root of one of the onions, sit it on its base, then make several deep cuts in the top to create a star shape, slicing about two-thirds of the way down the onion. Do the same with the other five onions, then divide the chilli butter equally among them, pushing it down into the cuts.

3   Put the onions in a small roasting tin, cover with foil and bake for 40–45 minutes until soft. About 5 minutes before they are ready, slice each goat's cheese in two, leaving the rind intact, then put on a baking sheet and bake for 2–3 minutes. To serve, put each onion on top of a piece of goat's cheese and drizzle with balsamic vinegar.

Serves 6	EASY		NUTRITIONAL INFORMATION	
	Preparation Time 15 minutes	**Cooking Time** 45 minutes	**Per Serving** 276 calories, 23g fat (of which 16g saturates), 5g carbohydrate, 0.9g salt	Vegetarian • Gluten free

Get Ahead

To prepare ahead Complete the recipe to the end of step 3, then cool, cover and chill for up to two days.
To use Complete the recipe.

Roasted Root Vegetable Salad

1 butternut squash, halved, seeded and cubed

1½ large carrots, cut into chunks

3 fresh thyme sprigs

1½ tbsp olive oil

2 red onions, cut into wedges

1 tbsp balsamic vinegar

400g can chickpeas, drained and rinsed

25g (1oz) pinenuts, toasted

100g (3½oz) wild rocket

salt and ground black pepper

1 Preheat the oven to 190°C (170°C fan oven) mark 5. Put the squash and carrots in a large deep roasting tin. Scatter over the thyme sprigs, drizzle with 1 tbsp oil and season with salt and pepper. Roast for 20 minutes.

2 Take the tin out of the oven, give it a good shake to make sure the vegetables aren't sticking, then add the onions. Drizzle the remaining oil over and toss to coat. Roast for a further 20 minutes or until all the vegetables are tender.

3 Remove the roasted vegetables from the oven and discard any twiggy sprigs of thyme. Drizzle the vinegar over, stir in and leave to cool.

4 To serve, put the chickpeas in a large serving bowl. Add the cooled vegetables, the pinenuts and rocket (reserving a few leaves to garnish). Toss everything together and garnish with the reserved rocket leaves.

EASY		NUTRITIONAL INFORMATION		Serves
Preparation Time 20 minutes, plus cooling	**Cooking Time** 40 minutes	**Per Serving** 290 calories, 14g fat (of which 2g saturates), 33g carbohydrate, 0.7g salt	Vegetarian Gluten free • Dairy free	**4**

Winter Coleslaw

4 oranges

400g can chickpeas, drained and rinsed

450g (1lb) carrots, coarsely grated

½ red cabbage, about 550g (1¼lb), finely shredded

75g (3oz) sultanas

6 tbsp freshly chopped coriander

4 tbsp extra virgin olive oil

3 tbsp red wine vinegar

salt and ground black pepper

1 Using a sharp knife, cut a thin slice of peel and pith from each end of the oranges. Put the oranges, cut side down, on a board and cut off the peel and pith. Remove any remaining pith. Cut out each segment, leaving the membrane behind. Squeeze the juice from the membrane into a bowl.

2 Put the orange segments and juice in a serving bowl with the chickpeas, carrots, cabbage, sultanas and coriander. Add the oil and vinegar, and season well with salt and pepper.

3 Toss everything together to coat thoroughly. Store the coleslaw in a sealable container in the refrigerator for up to two days.

Serves 6	EASY		NUTRITIONAL INFORMATION	
	Preparation Time 15 minutes		**Per Serving** 265 calories, 10g fat (of which 1g saturates), 38g carbohydrate, 0.4g salt	Vegetarian Gluten free • Dairy free

Get Ahead

To prepare ahead Complete the recipe up to the end of step 1. Put the cooled peppers in an airtight container, cover with olive oil, seal the container and chill for up to five days.
To use Complete the recipe.

4 red peppers, halved, cored and seeded

1 large red onion, thinly sliced

2 tbsp sunflower oil

1 head of chicory, thinly sliced

1 head of radicchio, shredded

150g (5oz) watercress, large stalks removed, roughly chopped

200g (7oz) mushrooms, thinly sliced

125g (4oz) pitted black olives, sliced

For the dressing

8 tbsp sunflower oil

2 tsp walnut oil

2 tbsp red wine vinegar

2 small shallots, very finely chopped

2 tsp caster sugar

Festive Salad

1 Put the red peppers skin side up on a baking sheet and cook under a hot grill until the skins are black and well charred. Transfer the peppers to a covered bowl or plastic bag and leave to cool. Remove the skins, roughly slice the flesh and set aside.

2 Brush the red onion slices with oil, then grill until tinged with brown. Leave to cool.

3 To make the dressing, whisk all the ingredients together in a bowl. Just before serving, put the chicory, radicchio, watercress, mushrooms, olives, peppers and onion in a large bowl, pour over the dressing and toss well. Transfer the salad to a serving dish and serve immediately.

EASY		NUTRITIONAL INFORMATION		Serves
Preparation Time 15 minutes, plus cooling	**Cooking Time** 15 minutes	**Per Serving** 205 calories, 17g fat (of which 2g saturates), 11g carbohydrate, 0.9g salt	Vegetarian Gluten free • Dairy free	8

Get Ahead

To prepare ahead Complete the recipe to the end of step 2 (but don't add the herbs to the vinaigrette), then cover and chill for up to two days.
To use Remove from the refrigerator up to 1 hour before serving, stir in the herbs and complete the recipe.

400g can mixed beans

400g can chickpeas

2 shallots, finely chopped

fresh mint sprigs and lemon zest to garnish

Mixed Beans with Lemon Vinaigrette

For the vinaigrette

2 tbsp lemon juice

2 tsp clear honey

8 tbsp extra virgin olive oil

3 tbsp freshly chopped mint

4 tbsp freshly chopped flat-leafed parsley

salt and ground black pepper

1 Put the drained beans and chickpeas in a serving bowl and add the shallots.

2 To make the vinaigrette, whisk together the lemon juice, honey and salt and pepper to taste. Gradually whisk in the oil and stir in the chopped herbs. Just before serving, pour the dressing over the bean mixture and toss well.

3 Transfer the salad to a serving dish, garnish with mint sprigs and lemon zest and serve immediately.

Serves	EASY	NUTRITIONAL INFORMATION	
6	**Preparation Time** 15 minutes	**Per Serving** 285 calories, 19g fat (of which 3g saturates), 22g carbohydrate, 1g salt	Vegetarian Gluten free • Dairy free

Freezing Tip

To freeze Complete the recipe to the end of step 2, then cool, wrap and freeze for up to one month.
To use Thaw overnight at cool room temperature. Cook at 200°C (180°C fan oven) mark 6 for 20–25 minutes or until piping hot to the centre.

Baked Potatoes with Mustard Seeds

6 baking potatoes, about 1.4kg (3lb), scrubbed
2 tbsp sunflower oil
1 tbsp coarse sea salt
4–5 large garlic cloves, unpeeled
50g (2oz) butter
6 tbsp crème fraîche
2 tbsp mustard seeds, toasted and lightly crushed
salt and ground black pepper
fresh oregano sprigs to garnish

1 Preheat the oven to 200°C (180°C fan oven) mark 6. Prick the potato skins all over with a fork, rub with oil and sprinkle with salt. Cook in the oven for 1 hour. Twenty minutes before the end of the cooking time, put the garlic cloves in a small roasting tin and cook for 20 minutes.

2 Squeeze the potatoes gently to check they are well cooked, then remove the potatoes and garlic from the oven and leave to cool slightly. When cool enough to handle, slice the tops off the potatoes and scoop the flesh into a warm bowl. Squeeze the garlic out of its skin and add it to the potato flesh with the butter, crème fraîche and mustard seeds. Season to taste with salt and pepper, then mash well. Return the potato mixture to the hollowed skins.

3 Put the filled potatoes on a baking sheet and return to the oven for 15 minutes or until golden brown. Garnish with oregano sprigs and serve hot.

EASY		NUTRITIONAL INFORMATION		Serves
Preparation Time 15–20 minutes	**Cooking Time** 1¼ hours	**Per Serving** 315 calories, 17g fat (of which 9g saturates), 38g carbohydrate, 1g salt	Vegetarian • Gluten free	**6**

4

Desserts, Bakes and Sweet Treats

Cranberry Christmas Pudding

200g (7oz) currants
200g (7oz) sultanas
200g (7oz) raisins
75g (3oz) dried cranberries or cherries
grated zest and juice of 1 orange
50ml (2fl oz) rum
50ml (2fl oz) brandy
1–2 tsp Angostura bitters
1 small apple, grated
1 carrot, grated
175g (6oz) fresh breadcrumbs
100g (3½oz) plain flour, sifted
1 tsp mixed spice
175g (6oz) light vegetarian suet
100g (3½oz) dark muscovado sugar
50g (2oz) blanched almonds, roughly chopped
2 medium eggs
butter to grease
fresh or frozen cranberries (thawed if frozen), fresh bay leaves and icing sugar to decorate
Brandy Butter (see page 15) to serve

1 Put the dried fruit, orange zest and juice in a large bowl. Pour over the rum, brandy and Angostura bitters. Cover and leave to soak in a cool place for at least 1 hour or overnight.

2 Add the apple, carrot, breadcrumbs, flour, mixed spice, suet, sugar, almonds and eggs to the bowl of soaked fruit. Use a wooden spoon to mix everything together well. Now's the time to make a wish!

3 Grease a 1.8 litre (3¼ pint) pudding basin and line with a 60cm (24in) square piece of muslin. Spoon the mixture into the prepared pudding basin and flatten the surface. Gather the muslin up and over the top, then twist and secure with string.

4 Put the basin on an upturned heatproof saucer or trivet in the base of a large pan. Pour in enough boiling water to come halfway up the side of the basin. Cover with a tight-fitting lid and simmer for 6 hours. Keep the water topped up. Remove the basin from the pan and leave to cool. When the pudding is cold, remove it from the basin, then wrap it in clingfilm and a double layer of foil. Store in a cool, dry place for up to six months.

5 To reheat, steam for 2½ hours; check the water level every 40 minutes and top up if necessary. Leave the pudding in the pan, covered, to keep warm until needed. Decorate with cranberries and bay leaves, dust with icing sugar. Serve with Brandy Butter.

EASY		NUTRITIONAL INFORMATION		Serves
Preparation Time 20 minutes, plus soaking	**Cooking Time** 6 hours	**Per Serving** 448 calories, 17g fat (of which 7g saturates), 68g carbohydrate, 0.3g salt	Vegetarian	**12**

Get Ahead

To prepare ahead Complete the recipe, cool, cover and chill for up to three days.

4 Williams or Comice pears

150g (5oz) granulated sugar

300ml (½ pint) red wine

150ml (¼ pint) sloe gin

1 cinnamon stick

zest of 1 orange

6 star anise

Greek yogurt or whipped cream to serve (optional)

Drunken Pears

1 Peel the pears, cut out the calyx at the base of each and leave the stalks intact. Put the sugar, wine, sloe gin and 300ml (½ pint) water in a small pan and heat gently until the sugar dissolves.

2 Bring to the boil and add the cinnamon stick, orange zest and star anise. Add the pears, then cover and poach over a low heat for 30 minutes or until tender.

3 Remove the pears with a slotted spoon, then continue to heat the liquid until it has reduced to about 200ml (7fl oz) or until syrupy. Pour the syrup over the pears. Serve warm or chilled with Greek yogurt or whipped cream, if you like.

Serves 4	EASY		NUTRITIONAL INFORMATION	
	Preparation Time 15 minutes	**Cooking Time** 50 minutes	**Per Serving** 305 calories, trace fat, 52g carbohydrate, 0g salt	Vegetarian Gluten free • Dairy free

Cook's Tip

Use thick-skinned oranges, such as navel oranges, as they are easier to peel.

Oranges with Caramel Sauce

6 oranges

25g (1oz) butter

2 tbsp golden caster sugar

2 tbsp Grand Marnier

2 tbsp marmalade

grated zest and juice of 1 large orange

crème fraîche to serve

1 Preheat the oven to 200°C (180°C fan oven) mark 6. Cut away the peel and pith from the oranges, then put them in a roasting tin just big enough to hold them.

2 Melt the butter in a pan and add the sugar, Grand Marnier, marmalade, orange zest and juice. Heat gently until the sugar dissolves. Pour the mixture over the oranges in the tin, then bake for 30–40 minutes until the oranges are caramelised. Serve warm with crème fraîche.

EASY		NUTRITIONAL INFORMATION		Serves
Preparation Time 15 minutes	**Cooking Time** 30–40 minutes	**Per Serving** 139 calories, 4g fat (of which 2g saturates), 24g carbohydrate, 0.1g salt	Vegetarian • Gluten free	**6**

Get Ahead

To prepare ahead Complete the recipe, cover and chill for up to two days.

Tropical Fruit and Coconut Trifle

1 small pineapple, roughly chopped

2 bananas, thickly sliced

2 x 400g cans mango slices in syrup, drained, syrup reserved

2 passion fruit, halved

175g (6oz) plain sponge, such as Madeira cake, roughly chopped

3 tbsp dark rum (optional)

200ml (7fl oz) coconut cream

500g carton fresh custard

500g carton Greek yogurt

600ml (1 pint) double cream

6 tbsp dark muscovado sugar

1 Put the pineapple pieces in a large trifle bowl, add the banana and mango slices and spoon over the passion fruit pulp. Top with the chopped sponge. Pour over the rum, if using, and 6 tbsp of the reserved mango syrup.

2 Mix together the coconut cream and custard and pour the mixture over the sponge.

3 Put the Greek yogurt and double cream in a bowl and whisk until thick. Spoon or pipe the mixture over the custard, then sprinkle with muscovado sugar. Cover and chill for at least 1 hour before serving.

Serves 16	EASY	NUTRITIONAL INFORMATION	
	Preparation Time 30 minutes, plus chilling	**Per Serving** 404 calories, 29g fat (of which 18g saturates), 33g carbohydrate, 0.2g salt	Vegetarian

Get Ahead

To prepare ahead Complete the recipe, cover and chill for up to two days.

125g (4oz) golden caster sugar

pared zest of 1 orange

5 sheets leaf gelatine

75cl bottle champagne or sparkling wine

2–3 tbsp orange-flavoured liqueur, such as Grand Marnier

edible gold leaf to decorate

Champagne Jellies

1 Put the sugar in a pan. Add the orange zest and 250ml (9fl oz) cold water. Heat gently until the sugar dissolves. Bring the mixture to the boil, then simmer gently for 2–3 minutes until slightly reduced and syrupy. Remove the pan from the heat and discard the orange zest.

2 Meanwhile, put the gelatine in a shallow bowl and cover with cold water. Leave to soak for 5 minutes.

3 Lift the gelatine out of the bowl, squeeze out excess water, then add it to the pan. Stir gently for 2–3 minutes until the gelatine dissolves completely.

4 Pour the champagne and liqueur into the pan, then transfer the mixture to a jug. Fill eight wine glasses with the jelly mixture, then chill for 4 hours or until set. Decorate with gold leaf to serve.

EASY		NUTRITIONAL INFORMATION		Serves
Preparation Time 15 minutes, plus chilling	**Cooking Time** 15 minutes	**Per Serving** 165 calories, trace fat, 21g carbohydrate, 0g salt	Gluten free • Dairy free	**8**

Get Ahead

Make this up to a month in advance and store in the freezer.

Cognac and Crème Fraîche Ice Cream

500g carton crème fraîche

175g (6oz) golden icing sugar, sifted

4 tbsp cognac

1 Line a 450g (1lb) loaf tin with clingfilm. Put the crème fraîche, icing sugar and cognac in a bowl and whisk well – the mixture will become thin, but continue whisking until it thickens slightly.

2 Pour the mixture into the lined tin, then cover and freeze for 6 hours.

3 To shape the ice-cream balls, dip an ice-cream scoop in a jug of boiling water before using.

Serves 8	EASY	NUTRITIONAL INFORMATION	
	Preparation Time 5 minutes, plus 6 hours freezing	**Per Serving** 339 calories, 25g fat (of which 17g saturates), 24g carbohydrate, 0g salt	Vegetarian • Gluten free

Cook's Tips

Sugared Redcurrants: dip a few sprigs of redcurrants in 1 large egg white, lightly beaten, then dip them in a little caster sugar. Shake off any excess sugar, then leave the redcurrants to harden on a baking sheet lined with greaseproof paper.

For an even more indulgent Christmas dessert, use clotted cream or Bailey's ice cream instead of vanilla.

Make this up to two weeks in advance and store in the freezer.

Cranberry Christmas Bombe

125g (4oz) granulated sugar

300ml (½ pint) cranberry juice

225g (8oz) each cranberries and raspberries, fresh or frozen

2 large egg whites

75g (3oz) caster sugar

groundnut oil to grease

500ml tub vanilla ice cream

Sugared Redcurrants (see Cook's Tip) to decorate

1 Put the granulated sugar and cranberry juice in a pan and heat gently until the sugar dissolves. Bring to the boil, then add the cranberries. Cover and simmer for 15 minutes until very soft. Leave to cool. Blend with the raspberries in a food processor or blender, press through a nylon sieve, then chill.

2 Whisk the egg whites until soft peaks form. Whisk in the caster sugar a spoonful at a time and continue whisking until stiff and glossy. Fold into the fruit purée. Pour into an ice-cream maker and churn until stiff.

3 Meanwhile, lightly oil a 1.4 litre (2½ pint) pudding basin, then put a disc of foil in the base. Put the basin in the freezer for 30 minutes. Spoon the cranberry sorbet into the basin, creating a hollow in the centre, and return to the freezer. Leave the vanilla ice cream at room temperature for 10 minutes. Spoon the ice cream into the centre of the sorbet and press down well. Freeze for 4 hours or until firm.

4 To unmould the bombe, dip the basin in hot water for 10 seconds, then loosen the edges with a round-bladed knife, invert on to a plate, shake firmly and remove the foil. Decorate with Sugared Redcurrants. Use a warm knife to cut the bombe into wedges.

A LITTLE EFFORT		NUTRITIONAL INFORMATION		Serves
Preparation Time 30 minutes, plus 6 hours chilling and freezing	**Cooking Time** 15 minutes	**Per Serving** 236 calories, 6g fat (of which 4g saturates), 44g carbohydrate, 0.1g salt	Vegetarian • Gluten Free	**8**

Christmas Cake

1kg (2¼lb) mixed dried fruit

100g (3½oz) ready-to-eat pitted prunes, roughly chopped

50g (2oz) ready-to-eat dried figs, roughly chopped

100g (3½oz) dried cranberries

2 balls preserved stem ginger in syrup, grated and syrup reserved

grated zest and juice of 1 orange

175ml (6fl oz) brandy

2 splashes Angostura bitters

175g (6oz) unsalted butter, cubed, plus extra to grease

175g (6oz) dark muscovado sugar

200g (7oz) self-raising flour

½ tsp ground cinnamon

½ tsp freshly grated nutmeg

½ tsp ground cloves

4 medium eggs, beaten

1 Preheat the oven to 150°C (130°C fan oven) mark 2. Grease and line the base and sides of a 20.5cm (8in) round, deep cake tin with greaseproof paper.

2 Put all the dried fruit in a very large pan and add the ginger, 1 tbsp reserved ginger syrup, orange zest and juice, brandy and Angostura bitters. Bring to the boil, then simmer for 5 minutes. Add the butter and sugar and heat gently to melt. Stir occasionally until the sugar dissolves.

3 Take the pan off the heat and leave to cool for a couple of minutes. Add the flour, spices and beaten egg and mix well.

4 Pour the mixture into the prepared tin and level the top. Wrap the outside of the tin in brown paper and secure with string to protect the cake during cooking. Bake for 2–2½ hours until the cake is firm to the touch. Test by inserting a skewer into the centre of the cake – it should come out clean.

5 Leave the cake to cool in the tin for 2–3 hours, then remove from the tin, leaving the greaseproof paper on, and leave to cool completely on a wire rack. Wrap the cake in a layer of clingfilm, then in foil. Store in an airtight container for up to three months.

Cook's Tip

After two weeks of maturing, prick the cake all over with a metal skewer and sprinkle over 1 tbsp brandy. Leave to soak in, then rewrap and store as before.

Makes 16 slices	EASY		NUTRITIONAL INFORMATION	
	Preparation Time 30 minutes	**Cooking Time** 2½ hours, plus cooling	**Per Slice** 277 calories, 11g fat (of which 6g saturates), 38g carbohydrate, 0.2g salt	Vegetarian

Get Ahead

The stollen will keep in an airtight container for up to one week – be sure to point this out if you are giving the second one as a gift.

To freeze Complete the recipe except for dusting with icing sugar. Wrap the stollen in clingfilm, put it in a freezer bag, label and freeze for up to three months.

To use Thaw at cool room temperature overnight, then dust with icing sugar.

Stollen

75g (3oz) fresh yeast, crumbled, or 40g (1½oz) dried yeast

700g (1½lb) plain flour, warmed in the microwave for 2 minutes on defrost, plus extra to dust

½ tsp ground coriander

¼ tsp ground nutmeg

100g (3½oz) caster sugar

2 medium eggs, beaten

250g (9oz) butter, softened

oil to grease

300g (11oz) raisins

125g (4oz) currants

150g (5oz) mixed candied peel, finely chopped

4 tbsp rum

grated zest of 1 large lemon

150g (5oz) blanched almonds, roughly chopped

1 tsp salt

250g pack white marzipan

250g (9oz) unsalted butter, melted

50g (2oz) icing sugar to dust

1 Mix together the yeast and 150ml (¼ pint) warm water. Put the flour and spices in a bowl and make a well in the centre. Pour in the yeast mixture and sprinkle with a little flour from the sides. Leave for 15 minutes or until the yeast bubbles. Mix the caster sugar and eggs in a separate bowl, then pour into the flour. Add the softened butter and mix until a rough dough forms. Turn out on to a lightly floured worksurface and knead for about 5 minutes until smooth. Put the dough in a lightly oiled bowl, cover with clingfilm and a clean teatowel and leave in a warm place for about 2 hours or until doubled in size.

2 Put the raisins, currants and mixed peel in a bowl and add the rum. Cover and set aside.

3 Turn the dough out on to a lightly floured worksurface and stretch it into a rough rectangle measuring about 35.5 x 25.5cm (14 x 10in). Tip the fruit into the middle of the dough, add the lemon zest, almonds and salt, then knead until the fruit and nuts are incorporated. Halve the marzipan and roll each piece into a sausage about 25.5cm (10in) long.

4 Cut the dough in half and shape into two ovals about 30.5cm (12in) long. Press a rolling pin lengthways down the middle of each to make a hollow and add the marzipan. Fold the dough over the marzipan, put on a baking sheet, then cover with clingfilm and a clean teatowel. Leave for 1 hour.

5 Preheat the oven to 180°C (160°C fan oven) mark 4. Bake for 35–45 minutes or until the loaves sound hollow when tapped on the base. Leave to cool for 15 minutes. Brush with the melted butter, using it all – this gives the bread a richer texture and helps keep it fresh. Dust with icing sugar before serving.

A LITTLE EFFORT		NUTRITIONAL INFORMATION		Makes
Preparation Time 40 minutes, plus 2 hours rising and 1 hour proving	**Cooking Time** about 45 minutes, plus cooling	**Per Serving, based on 12 slices per loaf** 343 calories, 23g fat (of which 11g saturates), 33g carbohydrate, 0.4g salt	Vegetarian	**2** loaves

Cook's Tips

Improve the flavour of a jar of bought mincemeat by adding 2 tbsp brandy, the grated zest of 1 lemon and 25g (1oz) pecan nuts, chopped. Instead of the nuts, try a piece of preserved stem ginger, chopped.

For vegetarians, make sure you use mincemeat made with vegetable suet rather than beef suet.

Mince Pies

225g (8oz) plain flour, plus extra to dust

125g (4oz) unsalted butter, chilled and diced

100g (3½oz) cream cheese

1 egg yolk

finely grated zest of 1 orange

1 egg, beaten

400g jar mincemeat (see Cook's Tips)

icing sugar to dust

1 Put the flour in a food processor. Add the butter, cream cheese, egg yolk and orange zest and whiz until the mixture just comes together. Tip the mixture into a large bowl and bring the dough together with your hands. Shape into a ball, wrap in clingfilm and put in the freezer for 5 minutes.

2 Preheat the oven to 220°C (200°C fan) mark 7. Cut off about one-third of the pastry dough and set aside. Roll out the remainder on a lightly floured worksurface to 5mm (¼in) thick. Stamp out circles with a 6.5cm (2½in) cutter to make 24 rounds, re-rolling the dough as necessary. Use the pastry circles to line two 12-hole patty tins. Roll out the reserved pastry and use a star cutter to stamp out the stars.

3 Put 1 tsp mincemeat into each pastry case, then top with pastry stars. Brush the tops with beaten egg, then bake for 12–15 minutes until golden. Remove from the tins and leave to cool on a wire rack. Serve warm or cold, dusted with icing sugar. Store in an airtight container for up to four days.

Makes 24	EASY		NUTRITIONAL INFORMATION	
	Preparation Time 15 minutes, plus chilling	**Cooking Time** 12–15 minutes	**Per Pie** 150 calories, 8g fat (of which 4g saturates), 17g carbohydrate, 0.2g salt	Vegetarian

Cook's Tip

Store the biscuits in an airtight container for up to one week.

To gift-wrap, pack the decorated biscuits in pretty boxes lined with greaseproof paper and attach a label with an eat-by date.

Spiced Star Biscuits

2 tbsp runny honey

25g (1oz) unsalted butter, plus extra to grease

50g (2oz) light muscovado sugar

finely grated zest of ½ lemon and ½ orange

225g (8oz) self-raising flour, plus extra to dust

1 tsp ground cinnamon

1 tsp ground ginger

½ tsp freshly grated nutmeg

a pinch of ground cloves

a pinch of salt

1 tbsp finely chopped candied peel

50g (2oz) ground almonds

1 large egg, beaten

1½–2 tbsp milk

150g (5oz) icing sugar and silver sugar balls to decorate

1. Put the honey, butter, sugar and citrus zests in a small pan and stir over a low heat until the butter has melted and the ingredients are well combined.

2. Sift the flour, spices and salt together into a bowl, then add the candied peel and ground almonds. Add the melted butter mixture, beaten egg and milk and mix until the dough comes together. Knead the dough briefly until smooth, then wrap it in clingfilm and chill for at least 4 hours, or overnight.

3. Preheat the oven to 180°C (160°C fan oven) mark 4. Roll out the dough on a lightly floured surface to 5mm (¼in) thick. Using a 5cm (2in) star cutter, stamp out stars and put on to greased baking sheets. Bake for 15–20 minutes until just beginning to brown at the edges. Transfer to a wire rack to cool.

4. To decorate, mix the icing sugar with 1½ tbsp warm water to make a smooth icing. Coat some of the biscuits with icing and pipe icing on to others, then decorate with silver balls. Leave the icing to set.

EASY		NUTRITIONAL INFORMATION		Makes
Preparation Time 15 minutes, plus 4 hours chilling	**Cooking Time** about 20 minutes, plus cooling	**Per Biscuit** 51 calories, 2g fat (of which 1g saturates), 8g carbohydrate, 0g salt	Vegetarian	**35**

Chocolate Mousse Roulade

6 large eggs, separated

150g (5oz) caster sugar, plus extra to sprinkle

50g (2oz) cocoa powder

frosted fruit and leaves to decorate (see page 22)

For the filling

225g (8oz) milk chocolate, roughly chopped

2 large eggs, separated

125g (4oz) fresh or frozen cranberries, halved

50g (2oz) granulated sugar

grated zest and juice of ½ medium orange

200ml (7fl oz) double cream

1 Preheat the oven to 180°C (160°C fan oven) mark 4. Line a 30.5 x 20.5cm (12 x 8in) Swiss roll tin with non-stick baking parchment – it needs to stick up around the edges of the tin by 5cm (2in) to allow the cake to rise.

2 First, make the filling. Put the chocolate in a large heatproof bowl and add 50ml (2fl oz) water. Place over a pan of gently simmering water, making sure the bowl doesn't touch the water. Leave to melt for 15–20 minutes. Remove the bowl from the heat and, without stirring, add the egg yolks, then stir until smooth. In a separate, grease-free bowl, whisk the egg whites until soft peaks form, then fold into the chocolate. Cover and chill for at least 2 hours.

3 Put the cranberries in a pan with the sugar, orange zest and juice, and 100ml (3½fl oz) water. Bring to a gentle simmer, then leave to barely simmer for 30 minutes, stirring occasionally until the cranberries are soft; there should be no excess liquid left in the pan. Remove from the heat and leave to cool.

4 To make the cake, put the egg yolks in a bowl and whisk with an electric hand whisk for 1–2 minutes until pale. Add the sugar and whisk until the mixture has the consistency of thick cream. Sift the cocoa powder over the mixture and fold in with a large metal spoon. In a separate, grease-free bowl, whisk the egg whites until soft peaks form. Stir a spoonful of the egg whites into the chocolate mixture to loosen it, then fold in the remainder. Pour the mixture into the prepared tin and bake for about 25 minutes or until well risen and spongy. Leave to cool completely in the tin (it will sink dramatically).

5 When cold, put a sheet of baking parchment on the worksurface and sprinkle with caster sugar. Turn the cake out on to the sugar and peel off the parchment. Spoon the chocolate filling on top and spread to within 2.5cm (1in) of the edge. Sprinkle over the glazed cranberries. Lightly whip the cream, spoon over the cranberries, then spread lightly to cover.

6 Holding a short edge of the baking parchment, gently lift and roll, pushing the edge down so it starts to curl. Keep lifting and rolling as the cake comes away from the paper. Don't worry if it cracks. Remove the paper. Chill for up to 8 hours. Decorate with frosted fruit and leaves.

Serves 8	FOR THE CONFIDENT COOK		NUTRITIONAL INFORMATION	
	Preparation Time 45 minutes, plus 2 hours chilling	**Cooking Time** 40 minutes, plus cooling	**Per Serving** 510 calories, 30g fat (of which 16g saturates), 53g carbohydrate, 0.4g salt	Vegetarian • Gluten free

Cook's Tips

Panforte is a flat Italian cake, a mixture of dried fruit and nuts, bound with honey and baked on rice paper. It is a Christmas speciality, so look for it in Italian delicatessens and larger supermarkets from November to January.
To freeze Complete the recipe but don't cut into slices. Wrap and freeze for up to three months.
To use Thaw at cool room temperature.

Chilled Chocolate Biscuit Cake

125g (4oz) butter, chopped, plus extra to grease

150g (5oz) plain chocolate, broken into pieces

250g (9oz) panforte, finely chopped

100g (3½oz) cantuccini biscuits or Rich Tea biscuits, finely chopped

2–3 tbsp Amaretto, rum or brandy

1 Grease an 18cm (7in) square cake tin and line the base with baking parchment. Put the butter and chocolate in a heatproof bowl over a pan of gently simmering water, taking care not to let the bowl touch the water. Stir until melted and set aside.

2 In a large bowl, mix the panforte, cantuccini or Rich Tea biscuits and liqueur, rum or brandy. Add the chocolate mixture and stir to coat.

3 Pour the mixture into the cake tin and chill for at least 2 hours. Cut into squares to serve.

Makes 16	EASY		NUTRITIONAL INFORMATION	
	Preparation Time 15 minutes, plus 2 hours chilling	**Cooking Time** 5 minutes	**Per Square** 206 calories, 12g fat (of which 7g saturates), 22g carbohydrate, 0.4g salt	Vegetarian

Get Ahead

Store the truffles in an airtight container in the refrigerator for up to two weeks.

Nutty Chocolate Truffles

100g (3½oz) hazelnuts

200g (7oz) plain chocolate (minimum 50% cocoa solids), broken into pieces

25g (1oz) butter

150ml (¼ pint) double cream

3 tbsp cocoa powder, sifted

3 tbsp golden icing sugar, sifted

1 Put the hazelnuts in a frying pan and heat gently for 3–4 minutes, shaking the pan occasionally, until toasted all over. Put 30 nuts in a bowl and leave to cool. Whiz the remaining nuts in a food processor until finely chopped. Put the chopped nuts in a shallow dish.

2 Melt the chocolate in a heatproof bowl over a pan of gently simmering water, taking care not to let the bowl touch the water. In a separate pan, melt the butter and cream. Bring just to the boil, then remove from the heat. Carefully stir into the chocolate. Whisk until cool and thick, then chill for 1–2 hours.

3 Put the cocoa powder and icing sugar in separate shallow dishes. Scoop up a teaspoonful of the chilled truffle mixture and push a hazelnut into the centre. Working quickly, shape into a ball, then roll in cocoa powder, icing sugar or chopped nuts. Repeat with the remaining truffle mixture, then chill until ready to serve.

EASY		NUTRITIONAL INFORMATION		Makes
Preparation Time 20 minutes, plus 1–2 hours chilling	**Cooking Time** 12 minutes	**Per Truffle** 96 calories, 8g fat (of which 4g saturates), 6g carbohydrate, 0.1g salt	Vegetarian • Gluten free	**30**

Cook's Tip

Serve these sweet squares with coffee after dinner.

Caramel Custard Squares

vegetable oil to grease

50g (2oz) granulated sugar

75g (3oz) golden caster sugar

1 tsp vanilla extract

6 large egg yolks

1 Preheat the oven to 170°C (150°C fan oven) mark 3. Lightly grease a 450g (1lb) loaf tin and line the base with baking parchment.

2 Put the granulated sugar in a small pan and heat gently until dissolved. Bring to the boil and cook for 2–3 minutes, tilting the pan but not stirring until it turns a golden caramel. Pour into the prepared tin.

3 Put the caster sugar in a pan with 75ml (2½fl oz) cold water and the vanilla extract. Heat gently until the sugar dissolves. Increase the heat and boil for 3 minutes or until syrupy. Leave to cool for 5 minutes.

4 Put the egg yolks in a large bowl and gradually stir in the cooled sugar syrup with a wooden spoon. Strain through a metal sieve into the loaf tin on to the caramel. Pour 2.5cm (1in) boiling water into a roasting tin, then rest a wire rack on top. Sit the loaf tin on the rack and cover the whole roasting tin with foil. Bake for 25 minutes until just firm and a skewer inserted into the centre comes out clean. Leave until cool, then chill for up to two days.

5 To serve, dip the base of the tin into a shallow dish of boiling water for 10 seconds. Run a sharp knife around the custard to loosen, then upturn on to a serving dish – there may be some caramel left in the tin but don't worry. Cut into eight squares and serve in petit four cases.

Makes	A LITTLE EFFORT		NUTRITIONAL INFORMATION	
8	**Preparation Time** 20 minutes, plus cooling and chilling	**Cooking Time** 30 minutes	**Per Square** 105 calories, 4g fat (of which 1g saturates), 16g carbohydrate, 0g salt	Vegetarian Gluten free • Dairy free

Cook's Tip

Store the fudge in an airtight container in the refrigerator for up to two weeks.

To make a gift, wrap piles of the fudge in clear cellophane and tie with a pretty ribbon, then attach a label to each parcel with an eat-by date and a note that the fudge should be stored in the refrigerator.

Cookies and Cream Fudge

sunflower oil to grease

125g (4oz) unsalted butter

200ml (7fl oz) evaporated milk

450g (1lb) golden caster sugar

1 tsp vanilla extract

75g (3oz) plain chocolate, chopped

25g (1oz) hazelnuts, toasted and roughly chopped

6 bourbon biscuits or Oreo cookies, roughly chopped

1 Lightly grease a 450g (1lb) loaf tin. Put the butter, evaporated milk, sugar, vanilla extract and 50ml (2fl oz) water in a large heavy-based pan, set over a low heat and stir until the butter has melted and the sugar dissolved. Increase the heat and boil gently for about 10 minutes, stirring all the time, until the mixture forms a soft ball when half a teaspoonful is dropped into a cup of cold water. Remove the pan from the heat and, working quickly, divide the fudge mixture between two bowls. Add the chocolate to one of the bowls, and allow it to melt into the fudge. Stir the mixture gently until smooth.

2 Pour half the chocolate fudge into the tin and smooth the surface, then scatter over half the hazelnuts and half the biscuits.

3 Pour the vanilla fudge into the tin, then top with the remaining nuts and biscuits. Finish with a layer of the chocolate fudge and set aside to cool. Cover with clingfilm and chill overnight. Cut the fudge into slices, then chop into 36 pieces.

EASY		NUTRITIONAL INFORMATION		Makes
Preparation Time 10 minutes, plus cooling and overnight chilling	**Cooking Time** 15 minutes	**Per Piece** 81 calories, 2g fat (of which 1g saturates), 17g carbohydrate, 0.1g salt	Vegetarian	**36**

5

Drinks

Mulled Wine

2 oranges
6 cloves
75cl bottle fruity red wine
2 measures (50ml) brandy or Cointreau
1 cinnamon stick, broken
½ tsp mixed spice
2 tbsp golden granulated sugar

1 Cut one of the oranges into six wedges and push a clove into each wedge. Using a vegetable peeler, carefully pare the zest of the other orange into strips.

2 Put the clove-studded orange wedges in a stainless-steel pan, along with the red wine, brandy or Cointreau, cinnamon stick, mixed spice and sugar. Warm gently over a low heat for 10–15 minutes, then remove the pan from the heat and set aside for 10 minutes to let the flavours infuse.

3 Strain the wine into a serving jug through a non-metallic sieve to remove the orange wedges and the cinnamon. Serve in heatproof glasses with a strip of orange zest draped over each glass.

Cook's Tip

Choose a bold, fruity red – nothing too oaky – such as Bordeaux or another wine made from Cabernet Sauvignon or Merlot.

EASY		NUTRITIONAL INFORMATION		Serves
Preparation Time 10 minutes, plus infusing	**Cooking Time** 10–15 minutes	**Per Serving** 120 calories, 0g fat, 5g carbohydrate, 0g salt	Vegetarian Gluten free • Dairy free	**6**

Try Something Different

Classic Champagne Cocktail: put a sugar cube in each glass, add 2 drops Angostura bitters and 2 tsp brandy. Top up with chilled champagne.

Champagne Cocktail

125ml (4fl oz) Grand Marnier

75ml (2½fl oz) grenadine

1 large orange, cut into 8 wedges

8 sugar cubes or sugar sticks

75cl bottle champagne, cava or other sparkling wine, chilled

1 Measure out the Grand Marnier and grenadine and divide among eight champagne glasses. Add an orange wedge and a sugar cube or stick to each glass.

2 Top up the glasses with the champagne, cava or sparkling wine and serve immediately.

Serves 8	EASY	NUTRITIONAL INFORMATION	
	Preparation Time 5 minutes	**Per Serving** 134 calories, 0g fat, 16g carbohydrate, 0g salt	Vegetarian Gluten free • Dairy free

Brandy Cocktail

4–5 ice cubes

1 measure (25ml) brandy

½ measure (12.5ml) Cointreau

1 dash Angostura bitters

1 Put the ice cubes in a brandy glass, then pour in the brandy, Cointreau and Angostura bitters.

2 Swirl around to chill, then, if you like, to avoid diluting the cocktail, lift out the ice with a slotted spoon and discard. Serve immediately.

Rum Punch

juice of 1 lime

2 tsp golden caster sugar

2 measures (50ml) dark rum

1 dash Angostura bitters

4–5 ice cubes

soda or mineral water, chilled

lime slices

1 Mix the lime juice and sugar in a tall glass. Add the rum, Angostura bitters and ice cubes.

2 Top up with soda or mineral water, add some slices of lime and serve immediately.

EASY	NUTRITIONAL INFORMATION		Serves
Preparation Time 2 minutes	**Per Serving** Brandy Cocktail: 96 calories, 0g fat, 5g carbohydrate, 0g salt Rum Punch: 143 calories, 0g fat, 8g carbohydrate, 0g salt	Vegetarian Gluten free • Dairy free	**4**

Try Something Different

Use pomegranate juice instead of cranberry, and add a spoonful of fresh pomegranate seeds to each glass instead of orange slices.

Cranberry Crush

75cl bottle sparkling wine, such as cava, chilled

300ml (½ pint) Calvados

1 litre (1¾ pints) cranberry juice, chilled

450ml (¾ pint) sparkling water, chilled

1 small orange, thinly sliced into rounds

ice cubes

1 Pour the sparkling wine, Calvados and cranberry juice into a large glass bowl.

2 Just before serving, pour in the sparkling water, stir, then add the orange slices and 10–12 ice cubes. Ladle into glasses and serve immediately.

Serves 14	EASY		NUTRITIONAL INFORMATION	
	Preparation Time 5 minutes		**Per Serving** 114 calories, 0g fat, 10g carbohydrate, 0g salt	Vegetarian Gluten free • Dairy free

Singapore Sling

1 measure (25ml) gin
2 measures (50ml) cherry brandy
juice of ½ lime
1–2 drops of Angostura bitters (optional)
ice cubes
1 cocktail cherry (optional)
150ml (¼ pint) soda water, chilled

1 Mix the gin, cherry brandy, lime juice and Angostura bitters, if using – this will give the drink an extra kick. Pour into a glass.

2 Add ice cubes and a cocktail cherry, if using, then top up with the soda water. Serve immediately.

EASY	NUTRITIONAL INFORMATION		Serves
Preparation Time 2 minutes	**Per Serving** 183 calories, 0g fat, 16g carbohydrate, 0g salt	Vegetarian Gluten free • Dairy free	1

Try Something Different

Virgin Mary: omit the vodka for a non-alcoholic cocktail.

Bloody Mary

1 tbsp Worcestershire sauce
1 dash Tabasco
1 measure (25ml) vodka, chilled
150ml (¼ pint) tomato juice, chilled
ice cubes
lemon juice to taste
celery salt to taste
1 celery stick, with the leaves left on, to serve

1 Pour the Worcestershire sauce, Tabasco, vodka and tomato juice into a tall glass and stir.

2 Add ice cubes and the lemon juice and celery salt to taste. Put the celery stick in the glass and serve.

Serves 4	EASY	NUTRITIONAL INFORMATION	
	Preparation Time 2 minutes	**Per Serving** 96 calories, 0g fat, 9g carbohydrate, 1.8g salt	Gluten free • Dairy free

Cook's Tip

Star fruit, also known as carambola, thinly sliced, makes a pretty garnish for drinks and desserts.

Fruity Punch

1 litre (1³/₄ pints) apple juice, chilled

1 litre (1³/₄ pints) ginger ale, chilled

2 apples, sliced and cut into stars, or star fruit (see Cook's Tip), thinly sliced

1 Put the apple juice, ginger ale and apple shapes in a large bowl and mix well.

2 Pour into a large jug and serve.

EASY	NUTRITIONAL INFORMATION		Serves
Preparation Time 5 minutes	**Per Serving** 66 calories, 0g fat, 17g carbohydrate, 0g salt	Vegetarian Gluten free • Dairy free	**8**

Cranberry Cooler

ice cubes

75ml (2¹/₂fl oz) cranberry juice

lemonade or sparkling water, chilled

1 lemon slice to serve

1 Half-fill a tall glass with ice and pour in the cranberry juice.

2 Top up with lemonade. If you'd prefer the drink to be less sweet, double the amount of cranberry juice and top up with sparkling water. Stir well and serve with a slice of lemon.

Serves 1	EASY	NUTRITIONAL INFORMATION	
	Preparation Time 2 minutes	**Per Serving** 29 calories, 0g fat, 7g carbohydrate, 0g salt	Vegetarian Gluten free • Dairy free

Glossary

Al dente Italian term commonly used to describe foods, especially pasta and vegetables, which are cooked until tender but still firm to the bite.

Baking blind Pre-baking a pastry case before filling to give a crisp result. Prick the pastry with a fork, then cover with greaseproof paper and weigh down with dried beans or ceramic baking beans. Bake for 10–15 minutes, then remove the paper and beans and bake for a further 10–15 minutes until the pastry is light golden and crisp.

Baste To spoon the juices and melted fat over meat, poultry, game or vegetables during roasting to keep them moist. The term is also used to describe spooning a marinade over something.

Beat To incorporate air into an ingredient or mixture by agitating it vigorously with a spoon, fork, whisk or electric mixer. The technique is also used to soften ingredients.

Bind To mix beaten egg or other liquid into a dry mixture to hold it together.

Blanch To immerse food briefly in fast-boiling water to loosen skins, such as tomatoes, or to remove bitterness, or to destroy enzymes and preserve the colour, flavour and texture of vegetables (especially prior to freezing).

Bouquet garni Small bunch of herbs – usually a mixture of parsley stems, thyme and a bay leaf – tied in muslin and used to flavour stocks, soups and stews.

Braise To cook meat, poultry, game or vegetables slowly in a small amount of liquid in a pan or casserole with a tight-fitting lid. The food is usually first browned in oil or fat.

Chill To cool food in the refrigerator.

Compote Fresh or dried fruit stewed in sugar syrup.

Coulis A smooth fruit or vegetable purée, thinned if necessary to a pouring consistency.

Cream To beat together fat and sugar until the mixture is pale and fluffy, and resembles whipped cream in texture and colour. The method is used in cakes and puddings that contain a high proportion of fat and require the incorporation of a lot of air.

Croûtons Small pieces of fried or toasted bread, served with soups and salads.

Crudités Raw vegetables, usually cut into slices or sticks, typically served with a dipping sauce.

Curdle To cause sauces or creamed mixtures to separate, usually by overheating or over-beating.

Cure To preserve fish, meat or poultry by smoking, drying or salting.

Deglaze To heat stock, wine or other liquid with the cooking juices left in the pan after roasting or sautéeing, scraping and stirring vigorously to dissolve the sediment on the bottom of the pan.

Dice To cut food into small cubes.

Dredge To sprinkle food generously with flour, sugar, icing sugar etc.

Dust To sprinkle lightly with flour, cornflour, icing sugar etc.

Escalope Thin slice of meat, such as pork, veal or turkey, from the top of the leg, usually pan-fried.

Fillet Term used to describe boned breasts of birds, boned sides of fish, and the undercut of a loin of beef, lamb, pork or veal.

Flake To separate food, such as cooked fish, into natural pieces.

Fry To cook food in hot fat or oil. There are various methods: shallow-frying in a little fat in a shallow pan; deep-frying, where the food is totally immersed in oil; dry-frying, in which fatty foods are cooked in a non-stick pan without extra fat; see also Stir-frying.

Garnish A decoration, usually edible, such as parsley, which is used to enhance the appearance of a savoury dish.

Gluten A protein constituent of grains, such as wheat and rye, which develops when the flour is mixed with water to give the dough elasticity.

Hull To remove the stalk and calyx from soft fruits, such as strawberries.

Infuse To immerse flavourings, such as aromatic vegetables, herbs, spices or vanilla, in a liquid to impart flavour. Usually the infused liquid is brought to the boil, then left to stand for a while.

Julienne Fine 'matchstick' strips of vegetables or citrus zest, sometimes used as a garnish.

Macerate To soften and flavour raw or dried foods by soaking in a liquid, eg soaking fruit in alcohol.

Marinate To soak raw meat, poultry or game – usually in a mixture of oil, wine, vinegar and flavourings – to soften and impart flavour. The mixture, which is known as a marinade, may be used to baste the food during cooking.

Medallion Small round piece of meat, usually beef or veal.

Mince To cut food into very fine pieces, using a mincer, food processor or knife.

Parboil To boil food for part of its cooking time before finishing it by another method.

Pare To finely peel the skin or zest from vegetables or fruit.

Poach To cook food gently in liquid at simmering point; the surface should be just trembling.

Pot-roast To cook meat in a covered pan with some fat and a little liquid.

Purée To pound, sieve or liquidise vegetables, fish or fruit to a smooth pulp. Purées often form the basis for soups and sauces.

Reduce To fast-boil stock or other liquid in an uncovered pan to evaporate water and concentrate the flavour.

Refresh To cool hot vegetables very quickly by plunging into ice-cold water or holding under cold running water in order to stop the cooking process and preserve the colour.

Roast To cook food by dry heat in the oven.

Roux A mixture of equal quantities of butter (or other fat) and flour cooked together to form the basis of many sauces.

Salsa Piquant sauce made from chopped fresh vegetables and sometimes fruit.

Sauté To cook food in a small quantity of fat over a high heat, shaking the pan constantly – usually in a sauté pan (a frying pan with straight sides and a wide base).

Scald To pour boiling water over food to clean it, or loosen skin, eg tomatoes. Also used to describe heating milk to just below boiling point.

Score To cut parallel lines in the surface of food, such as fish (or the fat layer on meat), to improve its appearance or help it cook more quickly.

Sear To brown meat quickly in a little hot fat before grilling or roasting.

Seasoned flour Flour mixed with a little salt and pepper, used for dusting meat, fish etc., before frying.

Shred To grate cheese or slice vegetables into very fine pieces or strips.

Sieve To press food through a sieve to obtain a smooth texture.

Sift To shake dry ingredients through a sieve to remove lumps.

Simmer To keep a liquid just below boiling point.

Skim To remove froth, scum or fat from the surface of stock, gravy, stews etc. Use either a skimmer, a spoon or kitchen paper.

Steam To cook food in steam, usually in a steamer over rapidly boiling water.

Steep To immerse food in warm or cold liquid to soften it, and sometimes to draw out strong flavours.

Stew To cook food, such as tougher cuts of meat, in flavoured liquid which is kept at simmering point.

Stir-fry To cook small, even-sized pieces of food rapidly in a little fat, tossing constantly over a high heat.

Sweat To cook chopped or sliced vegetables in a little fat without liquid in a covered pan over a low heat to soften.

Tepid The term used to describe a temperature of approximately blood heat, ie 37°C (98.7°F).

Vanilla sugar Sugar in which a vanilla pod has been stored to impart its flavour.

Whipping (whisking) Beating air rapidly into a mixture either with a manual or electric whisk. Whipping usually refers to cream.

Zest The thin, coloured outer layer of citrus fruit, which can be removed in fine strips with a zester.

Index